A Journey into Yesterday

A JOURNEY INTO YESTERDAY

Alfreda Mossburg

Guardian BOOKS

Belleville, Ontario, Canada

A Journey into Yesterday

ISBN: 1-55306-414-3

For more information or to order additional copies, please contact:

Joni Griswold
12504 S. County Line Road W.
Roanoke, IN 46783 USA

Guardian Books is an imprint of *Essence Publishing,* a Christian Book Publisher dedicated to furthering the work of Christ through the written word. For more information, contact:
44 Moira Street West, Belleville, Ontario, Canada K8P 1S3.
Phone: 1-800-238-6376. Fax: (613) 962-3055.
E-mail: info@essencegroup.com
Internet: www.essencegroup.com

Printed in Canada
by

Guardian
B O O K S

Thank you to my family who made this book possible!
A big thank you to my dear granddaughter
who never gave up on me! Thank you, Joni, thank you!

Table of Contents

Meet Our Mom, the Author and Poet

Our mother has written short stories and poetry all her life. One of her biggest projects was her Christmas diary. Each year, until the later years when she just took notes to "get around to later," she would write about all the events of that particular year. For her kids, it was just something she did. We read her work and enjoyed her humor and seriousness, but never appreciated it until a granddaughter, Joni, recognized their value. It became Joni's dream to have a book printed containing her grandmother's works. The following is a result of that dream. It is divided into three sections. The first is the Christmas diary entitled "1930 ~The Years Between ~1980", followed by History and Prose and then the Poetry sections.

The diary marks fifty years of marriage for our parents, D. Elmer and H. Alfreda Dennis Mossburg, and begins with their wedding and honeymoon. It ends with the celebration of their fifty years together. The last part of the diary is a brief history of the Mossburg family, written by our father. The other sections of the book contains her poems and short stories, some written when she was just a teenager. Throughout the whole book you'll meet parents, grandparents, aunt and uncles, townspeople such as Howard the banker and Ray the deliveryman.

Our parents were born and raised in rural Indiana. They both graduated from high school—a bit unusual for the '20s. Most of their lives were spent in a little town of Markle where they first met and where they raised their four offspring.

Mother turned ninety-two years old on July 27, 2002. She stills drives her car, her weekly entertainment is donning her Dixon ZTR cap and mowing her yard on her Dixon ZTR mower. Nobody has ever seen as much beauty in a single flower than our mother; a robin has never had a greater friend. But moles that dig up her yard, beware! She has a shovel and knows how to use it! She is best known for her fruit pies and fried potatoes; housework is her known enemy. Her life's work was raising us kids.

Dad was a fourth-generation building contractor. He retired in 1971 and passed away in 1987.

This book is a family treasure. We are so happy to share it with you and hope you enjoy it.

The Mossburg "Kids"
Jerry, Linda, Kirby and Jim

– 1930 –
The Years Between
– 1980 –

1930

THIS IS OUR FIRST MARRIED CHRISTMAS TOGETHER. We are happy in the little home we have dreamed of for so long. Our families on both sides spent Christmas with us. Mom and Dad surprised us with a quarter of beef, and Elmer's parents gave us one dozen hens and a rooster. We were so proud to share our little home, and they seemed to be very proud of their young married kids, the first experience for both families.

We have a squirrel family just outside our kitchen window. We have fun watching them every morning while we eat breakfast. I think they know we are watching and perform for our benefit.

We are in debt $305 for our furniture, and are paying five dollars a month rent. We still owe a little bit on our car. It scares me when I think about being in debt so much, but Elmer is making thirty cents an hour so maybe we will soon get it all paid.

I have canned a lot of good things this summer—enough to fill the fruit cupboard upstairs. Everything looks so nice.

We were married September 20th and went to Turkey Run for our honeymoon. Howard borrowed a tent from the Boy Scouts and we camped out. We cooked on a canned heat stove and really had some good meals. The trails were so beautiful, but some of them were hard to climb. My resourceful husband went to the car and got a rope to help the less-agile climbers, one of which was me! The weather turned cold and we came home earlier than we had intended to. We stayed with Elmer's folks until our little home was ready to move into.

The sad time was when we took the old truck and brought all our things from my parents' home. Elmer's mother had a lot of old clothes, which we tore into strips. Elmer sewed the strips together on the sewing machine while I crocheted them into rugs. I had worked at General Electric in Fort Wayne for twenty-seven cents per hour and had saved some money. I took some of it and bought material to finish four comfort tops Elmer's mother had given us. At my home, I had been busy making sheets, pillowcases, dresser scarves, tablecloths and many other things for our home.

Mom and I had picked raspberries, which we canned and made into jelly. Whatever she and Elmer's mother canned was shared with us. All of our treasures were piled in the corner of my mother's downstairs bedroom and when we left with it all piled high in the old truck, my heart was sad for the home I was leaving. Looking back through my tears I saw my father, mother, three sisters and my grandmother all in a row waving a sad goodbye. (In this year of 1980, I know what was in their hearts, how badly they felt when, I, their first child left home). I was homesick many times, but was so happy with my new husband.

We had a lot to do before we moved into our home. The place hadn't been lived in for a long time and first thing we did was sweep up a pile of dead honeybees. I couldn't believe this was *my* home! The responsibility scared me a little, but as we began to get the place livable, I began to feel equal to the occasion!

I was so proud of my new gas stove! It was green and ivory, as was all our kitchen furniture. It had a hand pump on the side that had to be used when the flame burned low. Our Sellers cabinet was so beautiful. It had a flour bin and a space for our dishes at the top and a row of drawers and space for our pans below. I had hemmed a lot of feed sacks so I had one drawer full of dishtowels. The top drawer held our cutlery and the bottom drawer held cake pans, etc. For the two windows, I made curtains of white material dotted with green, and gathered them on a stout cord to hang at the windows. I wished that some day I might have curtain rods. Isn't it ironic that with all these beautiful things I had, I wanted even more? Our enamel-topped worktable was where I made good meals to please my husband. Our beautiful green-and-ivory breakfast set completed our kitchen.

Our living room was so pretty. We had bought a new rug and an "overstuffed" three-piece living room suite from Bergies at Warren. We already had a table Elmer had given me for my birthday and a little wicker stand that held a big ivy plant. We had a second-hand rug we put down for winter and rolled up our good one until spring. Our parents both had kerosene lamps, but we were very modern and bought a gasoline mantle lamp that gave a very bright light from where it hung from the center of the ceiling. We had a hook in the kitchen ceiling too, but when we retired for the night, we carried a kerosene lamp upstairs.

Our bedroom was warmed by a stovepipe, which came through the floor from the heating stove in the living room below. I was very proud of our four-poster bed, chest and dressing table. Our fruit cupboard, which Elmer had built, stood close to the chimney to keep our canned goods from freezing. My sewing machine stood by the window.

Elmer's mother rarely rearranged her furniture, but almost every week, I moved the furniture around. One night while I was still reading, Elmer went upstairs in the dark and I heard an awful commotion and some highly-seasoned words. I rushed up to see what was wrong. It seemed as though he thought he was ready to jump into bed, but had walked into the sewing machine and thought he had broken his toe! He looked so funny, but I had to swallow my laughter and sat down on the stair step to compose myself!

Our pretty crocheted rugs covered the bare floor. I was very proud of them. Our running water was what ran out when we lifted and lowered the handle on the pump outside the kitchen door. Our bathroom facility was a little wood building some distance from the house.

1931

We are very happy. Our fire burns brightly and we love to sit in its glow. We have read a lot of good books this winter, played carom, visited with friends, gone to church, sang together while Elmer played his guitar and listened to our new Spartan radio! It was so beautiful and expensive! We went to Bluffton one Saturday night and strolled into a store just to look at radios. The dealer convinced us we could afford one by using the "Easy Payment" plan. It cost a third as much as our whole three rooms of furniture, but the future looked rosy and those payments seemed far away on that Saturday night. Even the small amount of cash we owned ($7.35) failed to deter us from going in debt another $125! When the music died down with the battery, we realized how foolish we had been. We swore we would see this thing through some way but never, never, never again would we do anything so silly!

It has been a good summer and I have learned a lot of things, one of which is that you don't plant soup beans the first of April. Another is that an old hen will not sit until *she* is in the notion! When a hen is ready to set, she becomes "broody" and won't get off the nest. I didn't know all of that until later. When I was ready for her to set, I put nice clean straw in the nest and placed twelve eggs just right. Then I caught the hen I thought would make a suitable mother and placed her on the eggs very carefully. As soon as I let go of her, she headed for high timber and I had to catch another one. This time I held onto her until I thought she understood what I meant. I finally gave up. Elmer's mother explained the process to me, so I waited for the hen to say when!

I have learned something else too! I guess the honeymoon is over because we have had our first quarrel! I guess you couldn't really call it a "quarrel" because neither of us said much, but I got the message anyway. Every night, we carry our kerosene lamp upstairs and set it on the dressing table. It is the rule that the last one in bed puts out the light. Of course, I was always just a wee bit behind, but my husband, wanting always to be a kind and thoughtful husband, would crawl out of bed without a word and put out the light, although we both knew I was cheating.

Then the inevitable happened! One night when I insisted I was in bed first, he pushed me out and I was too stubborn to get back into bed unless he coaxed me and he wasn't about to coax me. He snoozed the night away under the warm covers and I bawled all night on the floor wrapped in a crocheted rug! We wasted two cents worth of kerosene. That's how I learned that marriage is a fifty-fifty proposition.

I also learned that when cigars are used to keep moths out of the rug, they aren't supposed to be smoked first! When I was ready to roll our good rug up for winter, Elmer's mother said that a half box of leftover, year-old wedding cigars would be plenty for a 9' x 12' rug. I had often heard it said when someone spilled ashes on a rug, "don't worry about it, they will keep the moths out," so I assumed the ashes were what did the trick. I puffed away with zest, but before my pile of mothproofing got very high, I was sick enough to die. I tore down the stairs and out the door and ran smack into my neighbor who had just raised his hand to knock. I don't know which of us jumped the highest, but I'll bet a dollar he thinks Elmer's wife is "that way."

I learned also that people can get pretty desperate when they are cold and hungry. Work has been very scarce for us and many people don't have any. We are going through what they call a "Depression." The big cities have soup lines for the hungry. Nearly all the banks have closed and many people lost everything they owned. It isn't a bit unusual to read where another millionaire committed suicide.

That's one advantage of being poor. You don't have to kill yourself to avoid your commitments. Not long ago, I looked out the window to watch for my husband. I always go out to meet him, but that evening when I looked out, I saw a man stealing a telephone pole. He had it sawed and loaded in his trailer and was gone before Elmer got home. I was scared to death because he was between us and the only other house on our mile. We have noticed several other poles missing on our road, so someone is using them to burn, I suppose.

I have learned to drive this summer. Mother and Grace got brave enough to ride with me, so we went to Warren one day. We hit a pig and knocked it silly. We kept right on going because I got so scared I forgot how to stop the car! On our return trip, we didn't see hide nor hair of him. He was probably hiding in the tall grass trying to figure out what happened to him.

Most of the time, we walk where we want to go because we never go very far. We go east to visit Emma Gaiser and Molly Grover, north to visit Peony Brinniman and back a lane to Rachel Lucky. We go south to visit Ada Neff and Flora Dolby. We did our visiting on Monday, because I was at Elmer's folks all day. I went early in the morning with my basket of laundry when Elmer went to work. His mother had the water boiling and we set to work with gusto, taking turns on the rock-a-bye washer. The rock-a-bye was a wonderful machine. It was such an improvement over the tub and washboard. My mother did her washing in water which had to be "broken." It was heated on the range and red seal lye was sprinkled in to soften it. The scum that raised to the top was skimmed off and the water dipped into the tub of dirty clothes. Homemade soap was used on the washboard and about every week, my mother's hands were sore and bleeding after the washing was done.

Anyone who wasn't done washing by noon was considered to be loafing on the job. We were always done and after a good meal, we set out on our visits. I've often wondered if it was to prove to everybody that we had *our* washing done.

When we came home, the clothes were folded or damped for next day's ironing, while Grace started supper. We were always invited to stay and I can't remember ever turning it down. I'll bet they got sick of us!

Elmer's folks are awfully good to me. They have shared so many things with us. Our fruit cupboard is full again, thanks to them. Our garden was worse this year than it was last year, if that is possible. We have our coal bought and paid for—enough to last us for the winter. Now I feel so safe and warm when the wind whistles down our chimney and the branches scrape against the roof. We are so comfortable and happy. We go to Warren to the library about once a week and to Mt. Zion for our groceries. The snow has been deep for a long time now. Christmas day was very beautiful. We spent it with both our families, but came home early because the roads were drifting shut. I love winter time and the snow, but most of all, I love our little house. Surely no one has ever been happier than I!

Guy Will and Edna Fahl were married July 3rd. They, with Garl Sparks and Edna's sister, Mildred, and their brother Ross and his wife Nellie, came to our house for all night. Nobody got much sleep. Most of the night was spent heckling the newlyweds. Next morning, we were up early and away to Turkey Run for their honeymoon! (Years later, Guy told everyone that we were all so "damned poor" that it took eight of us to go on one honeymoon.) We slept on the ground all night and everyone except Elmer got the awfulest mess of chiggers anyone ever had! Thanks to the little critters, none of us ever forgot July 4, 1931.

This fall I worked at the tomato factory in Warren. It was hard work but I enjoyed it. I got acquainted with a lot of girls that worked there too—Florence and Doretha Cole, Elizabeth Gepheart, Leila and Eileen Shafer and Margaret Poulson were the ones I became better acquainted with. We ate our lunch together and believe it or not we enjoyed tomatoes with our sandwiches! Of course we discussed the latest fashions and it seemed that most of us were hoping to earn enough money to buy a "Princess Eugena" hat, which cost the exorbitant price of $3.98! It amounted to a handful of felt that perched jauntily on the side of the head and tipped down over one eye. Along the east side if you were headed north was a lovely white plume which was beautiful along side of the black felt! I was able to buy mine just in time for the Bluffton Street Fair and was so happy. My husband was not a street fair goer and took me, protesting all the way. We made one fast trip down Main and Market Streets and he said, "There, now you have seen the fair! Are you ready to go home now?"—so we started home and I hadn't seen a soul who commented on my hat! As we turned into Main Street it started to sprinkle and before we reached the car it was a downpour! We were both soaked to the hide, and my beautiful Princess Eugena hat was a sorry mess! I have seen wet rooster tails look better than my beautiful white plume! When I jumped in the car and shut the door it got caught, and when I retrieved it, it was a broken thing never again to grace the head of the one who adored it.

I don't suppose I'll ever get to go to the Street Fair again.

1932

This Christmas, we are spending in our own home in Buckeye! Dad and Mother Mossburg's house burned in March. They were sitting in their living room reading the paper, when a neighbor ran in and told them their house was afire! They both ran upstairs to rescue whatever they could and were both trapped. They escaped through a window where helping hands caught them when they had to jump. They didn't save anything—all Mother and Grace's beautiful quilts were gone. I think this grieved her more than the loss of anything else. She had spent hours making them and it was a great loss. All the jars of canned food were destroyed, along with many irreplaceable articles. My high school class ring was one of them.

Elmer and I were totally unaware of it until a neighbor came and told us. Of course, we were shocked and hurried to get over there. It was a terribly cold day, and the car wouldn't start and our good neighbor took us over. There was nothing left but a pile of debris. My heart ached for them, they were so dazed and heartsick.

We took them home with us, but words were of little comfort to them. We were so thankful they had both gotten out alive.

Howard was in Adrian, Michigan, in college and didn't know of it until a letter reached him. Grace had just finished a "Star of Texas" quilt and Mother had made a "Double Wedding Ring" that was to have been ours.

When news got around about the disaster, people, out of the goodness of their hearts, began to share what they had and the folks received more than they could possibly use. They were so over-whelmed and grateful. They tried to call a halt, but things kept coming. They received furniture for three bedrooms, kitchen and living room. Another kind soul asked them to move into the empty house across the road from theirs until theirs could be rebuilt.

That's how we came to be in our own home this Christmas. Dad wanted to buy the old store building in Buckeye, but the owners wanted him to buy the house that stood beside it too. They were asking $650 for the whole thing. We had gone with him to look at it and I had gone to visit Aunt Em who lived just two doors away. Elmer came and got me and said his dad had something he wanted to talk over with us. He said it would make us a nice home and that he would give $200 for the store as our down payment, if we could borrow the rest.

With total assets of a little over three dollars in our pocket, we set out to borrow $450.

There was no money to loan. The banks that hadn't already closed their doors were in such dire circumstances; they had their fingers crossed that they could hold out until times got better.

When we went to report our hard luck to the owners, the mother of the owner, whose home it once was, said, "What's wrong with me loaning you the money? I have never heard anything but good about this boy and I would like to see young people in my old home!" We were so amazed, we couldn't speak, but her son-in-law nearly threw a shoe! She looked him in the eye and said, "I'll have you know I'm still capable of running my own business, and

I'm going to loan them the money!" She took care of that son-in-law in a hurry.

We cast backward glances at the home we were leaving, remembering the happy hours we had spent there and hoped for the same happiness in our new home. We moved on the first day of April and had trouble stretching three rooms of furniture to furnish nine rooms! We had five empty ones for a long time.

We have a nice barn, two chicken houses, an up ground cellar, and three acres including an orchard, but we are deeper in debt than ever!

We bought a cow with crooked legs from Jake France, but we had to pay fifteen dollars for her anyway. Elmer milks her in the morning while I get breakfast and I milk her at night. We put the milk in flat crocks and when the cream comes to the top, it is skimmed off and saved in as cool a place as possible. Then I carry it to the store and sell it. My check was eighty-six cents one week. I saved a little from it each week and had enough to buy my husband three red handkerchiefs for Christmas. He bought me a cream can, which I appreciate because I really needed it! We managed small gifts for our families too. There isn't any money except for necessities, but we made things for our dear ones. No matter how poor we are, I want to always have something to give.

Carl and Mildred were married in January. My old pals are all married now. What fun we have visiting each other, exchanging recipes and household hints. We so enjoy our adult status and are so worldly-wise that we actually pity unmarried couples.

1933

Work is still scarce and there is much misery in this great country of ours. I am very thankful to live in a place where we can have our own cow so we can have milk, butter and our own cottage cheese. We feed our pig and the chickens the whey and sour milk we can't use. We butchered our pig and have our own meat. I do my sewing and have patched the patches on Elmer's pants several times.

It isn't unusual to have a tramp knock at our door and ask for something to eat and we always share what we have. While we were tearing down the store building, the awfulest looking man stopped and after we had fed him, he asked me to bring him three glasses of water, three small potatoes and nine toothpicks. He said he would like to make us something for feeding him. He carved three perfect roses and from his pocket, drew out two little bottles of coloring. He left one rose white, but tinted one pink and the other yellow. I kept them for a long time. I always remembered that although he was so poor, he still had something to give.

A man stopped one day when Elmer was gone, but Amanda and Aunt Em were close so I wasn't afraid. He waited outside while

I fixed him something to eat and I looked a long time at the two pieces of chicken, a thigh and a neck, before I could part with the thigh I had saved for my own lunch, but I never tasted such a good neck. The good things in life are much better when they are shared.

Carl and Mary have bought the store here. It is so nice to have them near. Their first order of groceries was pretty skimpy. Mary and I helped put the ware on the shelf and set it all close to the edge so it would look like the shelf was really crowded.

We have spent a lot of time this year also making gifts for our families' Christmas. I made aprons for our mothers, Elmer made a magazine rack for Aunt Em and tie racks for Howard and our fathers. I made dollhouses with clothespin furniture for Mary and Marjorie. We bought bracelets for Dorothy and Grace, which was all the money we spent. Our tree was a little one, but it was pretty.

The most important thing we are working on is a bed for our baby who is to come sometime in April! Elmer bought a walnut log from Sherman Smith and had it sawed into pieces, which he will combine with some birds-eye maple. I know it will be pretty.

I am scared and will be glad when this is all over. It seems strange to think there will be three of us, but I can hardly wait to see it.

We sold our calf for seventeen dollars and my mom and dad went with us to Fort Wayne. Mom helped me choose what I would need for our baby.

I didn't have any money left, but I guess I have all the things I need. On the way home, Elmer said, "Gee, I didn't know it cost so much to have a baby!" Dad and Mom thought that was real funny, but I didn't know it would cost so much either.

I look at all the little things in the bottom drawer every day and can hardly wait. I think so much about Christmas next year when we will have our baby and all this suspense will be over. I have thought of a lot of boy and girl names, but none of them seem to be just right for my own. Guess I'll have to let him or her grow up and name him or her self!

When I was about four years old, I had a playmate who lived next door whose name was "Reno Bundenelle." His brother's name was "Ward Savilliard" and I thought they were beautiful names, but when I mentioned either of them, Elmer turned thumbs down. He liked the name "Edwin," but not me. When I was little, we used to visit some people and an "Edwin" would tease the life nearly out of me and I hated him. I wasn't going to name my little boy after that monster—in case it turned out to be a boy. *This* had to be a very special name.

We had some good luck. Elmer got a job husking corn for fifty cents a day. It will sure help.

When the trains stop here at the elevator, sometimes coal rolls off the coal cars. We take a sack and go down the tracks and have found quite a lot of coal. We carry corn cobs from the elevator to make our coal go farther. The cobs make a nice summer fire because they heat the stove fast and are soon burned out so the kitchen can cool off sooner. On canning days, a fire must be kept going at full speed and we nearly roast. (We didn't need a "sauna" in those days. We stood in one when we did our washing and ironing and our canning.)

We had a nice Christmas. We went to the Christmas program at Boehmer. We laughed at a little girl who was supposed to be very enthusiastic about a new doll. She just stood there and in a barely audible monotone voice forced out, "oh, oh, a new doll."

We spent Christmas Eve with Elmer's folks and Christmas Day with mine. Everybody is anxious for the new baby to come.

1934

It was a boy! His name isn't Reno or Ward or Edwin, it is *Jerry Allyn*. Dorothy and Grace wanted Jerry and I added the Allyn. Elmer was pleased with the choice too. Our dear little boy has red hair and blue eyes, and is a joy to the whole family. He got a lot more attention than the Christmas tree did.

His birth was difficult and Dr. Black said afterward he thought he was going to have to load me up and take me to the hospital, which was pretty scary because very few people went to the hospital and then, only as a last resort. (In the year 1934, the hospital was considered to be the jumping off place to the next world!)

I had my preparations made for his birth a long time in advance. Mom and Elmer's mother taught me the art of making bed pads out of old sheets and newspapers. His basket was made soft and warm with pretty blankets and a soft pillow. The baby oil, cotton, boric acid powders, Ivory soap and talcum all were ready and waiting.

When the time came, my blessed friends Mary Hunnicut and Emma Gaiser stood ready to help. They made me walk most of the night. Along with the pain, I thought I could not take one more

31

step—but with them on each side of me, I walked and walked and walked. Dr. Black came about 9:00 p.m. after Elmer called him. He gave us the sad news that he was going back to town because we wouldn't need him for hours yet. Those next ten hours were the worst of my life and I vowed "never again." The doctor returned about 7:00 the next morning and our baby wasn't born until after 11:00 a.m. When the doctor held him up, I was transported into a new world—the pain was almost forgotten as I saw my son for the first time, he was so pink and pink is my favorite color!

Amanda Foust had given me a china commode and the doctor placed the placenta in it. After the tense moments were over, I guess he thought it was time for a little levity and said, "Elmer, I think I dropped my scissors in that pot. Would you look for them for me?" as Elmer turned green and said, "Gee whiz, Doc, I can't do that." The doctor exploded with laughter and added, "Well, take that out and bury it then!" As Elmer disappeared around the corner carrying the thing at arm's length, the doctor nearly fell on his face laughing!

Later on when this receptacle was needed for other duties, my Aunt Nora, who came to take care of us, couldn't find it anywhere. She asked Elmer what he did with it and he replied that the doctor had told him to bury it. We thought he had until Aunt Nora found it empty at the back of the storage room off the porch!

When Emma went home to relieve "Grandma Mossburg," who stayed with her sick husband while she administered kindness and help to us, she gave the word that a son had been born. In a very short time, they came tearing down the driveway. I never saw anyone so relieved and happy. Grandmother wanted to do something for me and I said, "Get me something to eat, I'm nearly starved to death." An hour after Jerry was born, I ate a slice of ham, two eggs and a piece of toast!

Mom, Dad and the girls came the next day, which was Sunday. They, too, were very happy. They don't get to see him so often, but Grandpa and Grandma Mossburg come over almost every night to see him. I am so glad I could give them a gift like him. Elmer's mother is sixty-four and has waited a long time for her first grandchild.

Jerry got lots of nice presents when he came and also this, his first Christmas. Now I know how Mary felt when the Wise Men brought gifts to her little son.

1935

*O*ur little boy is twenty months old this Christmas. It was hard to keep the trim on the tree with a curious little boy around. We have a nice tree this year. Work has been picking up a little and we are making our payments on time.

Through the Depression, many people lost their farms. Most of them were terribly run down and many of them were owned by the Louisville Land Bank. A bank representative came one day and said Elmer had been recommended to do some work for them. He accepted immediately and was kept busy. He needed help, so he hired Carl (Johnny) Marshall and Ralph Poulson.

About a year before Jerry was born, I enlarged our small living room. We had discussed it often but it always got put off until "someday." I decided it didn't look like too hard a job, so I tackled it myself. I felt like anything I could do to save my husband's strength I should do. I got along fine and had the mess all cleaned up when Elmer and his dad came home. His dad said, "Gee whiz, Sis, you might have had the whole upstairs down on your head!" I was too smart for that because I had gone upstairs to see which way the flooring was laid before I started. I never thought to see if it was a double floor. Luckily for me, it wasn't.

Our kitchen was a dark room with a porch over the one window and once more, I "set-to" with the hammer and wrecking bar. Aunt Em kept Jerry all day and I had a job on my hands. Instead of two short walls, I had to tear out a stairway and demolish a pantry to get some light into my dungeon. Elmer had to help me finish it because I had started something I couldn't finish. I did learn the basics of how a house is put together, and stored the knowledge in case I might need it in future years.

Our kitchen isn't finished yet, but we have the new windows in. It is really nice to have a light room. Elmer will build cabinets across the north end when he has time. He must work on the job when he can for we need the money, but someday, my kitchen will be finished.

We spent Christmas with both our families, but came home early so we could put our tired little boy to bed.

Another Christmas is nearly over. It is such a happy time, I am always sorry when it is over. We are looking forward to the new year and wonder what is in store for us. All I ask for is protection for our young son, good health for him, his father and his mother.

1936

This Christmas finds us in our new kitchen. It is all finished and it is so beautiful. The cupboards are all along the north wall with a sink under the big windows. We have new linoleum and wallpaper. Howard helped me paint the woodwork, and Elmer did the papering. Everything is green and ivory.

We had a lot of good things happen this year. Our home is our own at last. Elmer got a check from the Land Bank for $150, which was more than enough to pay off our debt. We both took it over to Mandy and she was just as happy as we were. Her faith in us had not proven to be wrong.

The Land Bank had a job near North Manchester for the boys to do. Elmer wanted to take Jerry and me along so he would have a cook. We rounded up a tent and what we thought we would need to camp for the duration and with Ralph and Johnny, we headed for North Manchester.

Johnny and Ralph carried straw from the barn and made themselves a bed under a nice big tree. We took a cot for Jerry and made ourselves a bed on the ground inside the tent. All went well. I cooked three meals a day on a little two-burner oil stove. The boys dug a hole in the ground and put a big container in it with sand between it and the earth. We poured water in the sand each morning and this served as our cellar to keep our milk and butter cool.

Their favorite breakfast was pancakes and bacon, and one morning, one of them challenged the other to a pancake-eating contest. I don't remember who won, but I do remember I fried forty-three pancakes. Next morning when I asked them what they wanted for breakfast, Ralph said, "Anything but pancakes!"

They also built themselves a seat, as we didn't have any chairs. It was a very crude affair, but served the purpose. They argued over the ownership of it and decided that the first one married would get it for a wedding present.

One night after we had all bedded down for the night, a terrible storm came up suddenly. The fellows knew they'd better get out from under that tree. They dragged their straw and bedding inside the tent. Then the tent started to leak. We moved Jerry's cot under the ridgepole, which was the only spot that wasn't leaking like a sieve. The rest of us just "endured." Next morning, I was trying to prepare breakfast in the soppy mess when Ralph poured water out of his shoe and sat down beside the stove to put them on. Oil had leaked out of the stove down onto the bedding they had dragged in and somehow caught fire! So we fought fire. The trials of fire and flood dampened our enthusiasm for camping somewhat.

The wonderful weekend that followed more than made up for the misery we had been through. Johnny and Ralph went home and brought their girlfriends back. We went to the dunes in Michigan and had a wonderful time. The three men took up residence under the tree that night and we girls talked half the night away in the tent. Next morning while we were cleaning up camp after breakfast, Eileen asked what to put the bacon grease in and I told her where the bowl was that I used. We had had trouble with a dog that snooped around our camp and found that he had licked clean the bowl that Johnny had just eaten his cereal from.

Ralph and Mary were married in November and one Sunday, Johnny, Eileen, Elmer and I made a trip to North Manchester. On the night of the shower the neighborhood had for them, they couldn't imagine what could be in the over-sized package that had to be carried in by two men. When they tore open the well-wrapped article, imagine their surprise when they beheld the old bench from North Manchester.

Jerry's walker is now a "Kiddie car" and I'll bet he has gone 1,000 miles in it. When it is cold and he can't play outside, he rides his car around and around the heating stove singing, "Bringing in the sheaves." He enjoys the stories I read to him. His favorite is about "Little Brown Koko." When the magazine comes, he always wants to know what "Little Brown Koko" is doing now, so we have to find out.

One story was about how "Little Brown Koko's" big, fat mammy loved him so much that she went into her pretty kitchen, tied her big apron around her middle, took down a shiny pan and made "Little Brown Koko" some brown sugar fudge.

She took three cups brown sugar, one cup white sugar, one-cup cream, one-half cup butter and one-half cup white Karo and cooked it all together to form a soft ball in cold water. Then she added one-teaspoon vanilla and beat it until it was creamy. Then she added two cups chopped nuts and turned it out to cool. Little Brown Koko loved it and ate so much, he nearly made himself sick. Jerry sat there on my lap in deep thought and finally said, "I wish MY big, fat mammy would make ME some brown sugar fudge."

Need I tell you that recipe has been in my cookbook for forty-four years and is still made at Christmas time?

Dorothy and Darwin were married in June and are living in Fort Wayne. Mom and Dad still have half of their family. Mary is fourteen and Marjorie is twelve.

We spent Christmas with parents on both sides of the house. Our little boy had a lot of fun. He was hypnotized with the tree and spent a lot of time under and around it. My hope is that we will always be able to provide the things he will need with a little left over to buy the things he would like to have. My prayer this Christmas is for good health and happiness for our little family!

1937

This has been a wonderful year. The most important thing is that the early part of next year Jerry will have a little playmate! We have been going to Dr. Meade in Bluffton because my husband thinks it best for me to go to the hospital, and I think he is right.

This has been a bad, cold winter. We put our little boy to bed and spend lots of evenings playing dominoes. Carl and Mary have three now, so they don't run around much either. We can yell back and forth across the railroad track. Mary is expecting their fourth child and we have lots of "symptoms" to exchange with each other.

The impossible dreams have become possible this summer. The R.E.M.C. has been working in our area to bring electricity to our homes. Our house was wired and ready, and on the 23rd of September (Elmer's birthday), the miracle happened.

Our first investment was a washer and an iron. I had sometime before realized my dream of a rock-a-bye washer, but now it had to go! I was lucky to have a cistern full of good rainwater just outside the kitchen door so I didn't have far to carry wash water. We carry our drinking water from Amanda's and she and Aunt Em carry their wash water from our cistern.

The first time I used the washer, I left the lid off just so I could see all that hard work being done for me. The wringer was a thing of pure joy! It squeezed the water out much better than I could. The washer had a hose on it and after the washing was done, the water was drained out in a bucket and carried out. In order to get the last pennies worth out of the soap suds, wash day was also "scrub out the out-house day." The clothes were put through two rinses and then hung out to dry. The rinse water was used to scrub porches and walks. Then the fire in the cookstove was allowed to go out and the kitchen returned to its normal ninety degrees for the heat was no longer needed for the iron. Some things I took off the line and pressed to use the heat before the fire went completely out.

Tuesday was ironing day, but after breakfast, I could let the fire go out because of my wonderful new iron.

My work was made so much easier with the coming of electricity. I appreciated it doubly with the new baby coming. I reveled completely in my happiness because my mother and Elmer's also were enjoying the same blessings I was.

This was an "electric" Christmas. We received two toasters, two waffle irons, Jerry got two trains, and I am sure I will have two babies!

1938

anuary and February of this year were stormy and bad. The meaner the night, the more sure Elmer was that I would be on my way before morning. Finally, on February 13th, on a Sunday, I knew it was time to go. I went down to the store to tell Mary goodbye and she said, "If you don't have twins, I will sure miss my guess!"

I gathered the sweet baby things from the bottom drawer and wondered who would be wearing them home. Little Jerry followed me all over the house asking questions, mostly about when I was coming home! At that time, children were allowed in the hospital to see the new baby and mother. I promised him faithfully that his daddy would bring him to Bluffton to see me, and when we left, his little face was pressed to Aunt Em's window, and a very sad little face it was. His daddy assured me he would bring him up to see me the next day.

I had so much hoped for a little girl that I hadn't even bothered to choose a boy's name. My choice was Leila Eulala, and Elmer nearly had a fit! "I don't know where you find all those silly names! I can't even pronounce it!" So that was the end of Leila Eulala. His choice was Linda and I like it too.

About 2:30 p.m. on the 14th, Linda Gay was born. All during the ordeal, the doctor and nurses were talking about going bowling. They didn't seem nearly as interested in this project as I was and went about their duties as if they were only washing dishes! They whisked her away and I didn't get to see her until the next morning.

A nurse brought two babies in and asked me which one I wanted, and I choose the cutest one. She tried to convince me the other one was mine, but I knew better. She said, "It happens every time, I have never yet had a mother choose the wrong baby!"

My own was a little doll with dark red hair and dark eyes. I could hardly wait for Jerry to see his little sister, and then they lowered the boom! On account of a scarlet fever scare, they forbade any children to be brought into the hospital. I was heartsick because all I could think of was that little face pressed against the windowpane when we left home.

My room was close to the kitchen and I was getting hungrier by the minute. My breakfast wasn't worth remembering, but I decided to forgive them for from the delicious smells coming from the kitchen, I knew the noon meal would make up for it. The tray-bearing nurses flashed past my door and I could hardly wait! When my tray came, it held a cup of water they had dragged a tealeaf through, a bowl of water they had labeled broth and a dish of green Jell-O.

I bawled because I was so hungry and so homesick for Jerry. I didn't think I could possibly endure the next two days. I longed for home and for Grandma Mossburg who would fix me some ham and eggs!

1939

A lot of changes have taken place in our lives this year. Our dear friend and neighbor left us this spring and we miss her very much. Her wisdom always amazed me and I often wondered if I could ever be as well informed as she. She was witty and a lot of fun to be with. She loved our little boy and she was one of his favorite people. In fact, she was too good to him. For some time I had been worried because he never seemed to be hungry at lunch time and I mentioned it to her one day. She laughed and said, "Now, don't you scold him!" and proceeded to tell me what he had been up to. I knew that he ate a good breakfast with us at 5:30 because he always got up as soon as he heard us stirring. Amanda slept longer and ate her breakfast about 8:30, so he ate with her. Aunt Em got up early but never ate breakfast, so she ate at 11:00 and he made it a habit to "go see Aunt Em" and ate again! I told him he mustn't do that any more and the next morning Amanda said a timid little knock came on her back door. When she opened it Jerry said, "I can't come in your front door anymore!"

Amada was seventy-two when her life ended. She was living with Merlin and Esther and had become very frail. They had been up many hours day and night, so Mary H. and I went to relieve them. We knew she was very low and expected her to go any minute. I'll never forget that long, long night! The June bugs were thick and kept banging into the window. Every time they did I came up off my chair about a foot. I had a much different attitude about death in those days. Amanda died in the early morning and I lost a very good friend.

Time was when someone died, the funeral director came to the home and the body was taken care of there, and placed in the coffin which usually stood in the "parlor" (that was a room that contained the family's best furniture). The shades were always drawn and it was a dark and foreboding place. At my Grandma Burley's house, we were never allowed to go in there. Sometimes we opened the door a crack and gazed with awe at the long lace curtains, the fabric-covered, fringe-trimmed chairs, the claw-footed stand in the center of the room with the family Bible on top and a pink conch shell on the shelf beneath it, the Brussels carpet and the long-haired ancestors in pictures on the wall. The ancestors looked as stiff and unfriendly as the rest of the room and I was scared to death of them. The only time we were ever admitted into that room was when my Grandfather laid in there—dead. Then it was the custom for someone to spend the night in the home of the deceased, but I'll tell you it wasn't one of my favorite times. Elmer and I sat all night in the home of a neighbor after a death in the family. There are a lot of noises in the night that one is never aware of until attending a "wake." I didn't even trust my brave husband's protection although I cringed near him all night!

Ray and Fern Sills bought Amanda's home and moved to Buckeye. Fern became my close friend and we spent many happy hours together.

Ray started painting for Elmer on the houses in Fort Wayne.

Elmer and his crew built the second house built in Kirkwood Park. It was built for a Mr. Gettle who sold it to a well-known grocer who has about a dozen grocery stores bearing his name. He and his bride wanted some changes made in the house, which Elmer did. When he presented his bill for $100 it was ignored. One day Elmer saw him working in his yard and asked him if the work was satisfactory or the cost too high. He replied that everything was fine. When Elmer asked him to explain why he hadn't received his money the "gentleman" (?) said, "I don't figure it is enough to sue me for so I'm just not going to pay it"—and he never did! No matter how great this man becomes or the extent of his philanthropic contributions it will never do him a bit of good as far as furthering his chances of a place in glory because he cheated an honest man of what he owed him.

Most of the people he worked for were fine people but one like this man was one too many!

We were very busy people this summer. Elmer's work was very demanding. He had gone into the business with two other men— one was supposed to sell lots, one was supposed to do the contact work of selling houses to be built and Elmer was supposed to build the houses. The partnership wasn't very old before Elmer was doing most of it himself. The one partner found he needed to go to the lake to "get away from it all," the other one was inebriated half the time, and so people starting coming to Elmer for the whole thing. (I have often wished he had stayed in the work that he had been doing. He changed from a carefree, happy person to an over-worked one determined to make a go of what he had committed himself to. I'll always believe the tension and frustrations were prime contributor to his high blood pressure which developed in later years.)

Christmas time was a nice time. We gave a party for the seven fellows who had worked so faithfully all summer. They and their families plus Elmer's folks, Howard and Grace made a pretty full table at suppertime. We had such a good time that the hard work I had done was well worthwhile.

Someone told Elmer one time that if he expected to be a success in his business, he should stop fraternizing with his help! We never knew whether or not that man was a great success in life, but we have derived much happiness from friendships of the people who worked with him.

At Christmas time Ray helped Elmer carry in my present. It was a beautiful electric range! I was so surprised I ran back to the bedroom and bawled. Now I no longer needed to have a fire in the coal range on a boiling hot day! How long would these blessings keep showering down on me?

The brown sugar fudge I made for Little Brown Koko was a breeze to make on my new stove!

We spent Christmas with both our families. Ours are the only grandchildren on either side of the family and we could never deny them the pleasure of sharing the little ones.

Another year will soon be ending and in my earnest prayers I ask for good health for us all and strength for my husband in the work he has undertaken. I ask that if great success does come to him that we will stay the same as we are. I enjoy the things that money can buy, but not if it is to change our lives to the point that "things" mean more to us than we mean to each other.

1940

oon after Christmas last year I developed a terrible sore throat. Fern came over and said she was going to paint my throat with Mercurochrome. I gagged and snorted around 'til she was ready to throw in the towel. She said "You big baby, now stop that!" but no matter how hard I tried, I still gagged. She nearly had to pin me to the floor but she painted my throat. The next morning I told her it was much better but I was still terribly sick at my stomach and blamed her and her throat swab. My throat healed in record time but the sickness didn't go away. I finally came to realize my trouble was caused by something that time alone would take care of. We were pregnant again! When I told Fern she said, "And you were blaming *me*!"

Ray and Fern moved from Buckeye temporarily to stay with his mother after his father died but we see them often. Fern doesn't have an electric washer and said she would do my washing if she could do hers on our machine. That worked out fine for both of us and we had a lot of fun besides.

Early in the spring I decided that with a new baby coming, we would need to expand our living quarters. I started working upstairs, scrubbing, painting and plastering. I called a paperhanger and he surveyed the job to be done and said, "If I can just paper as crooked as you can plaster we might have a pretty good-looking job here!"

I tried to hang a door and it looked worse than my plastering. I couldn't open it and walk through without holding on to it unless I didn't mind getting slapped on the backside by it.

The day finally came when I was ready to move upstairs and together Fern and I pushed and pulled 'til we got my mission accomplished.

Elmer spent so little time at home he was hardly aware of what was going on and that night was pretty surprised when he found his bed missing from its customary spot!

Jerry and Linda's room was so pretty. I made blue and peach bedspreads for their new twin beds and curtains from the same type material.

I loved the wallpaper in our room. It was pink with a white eyelet print laced in blue. I made scarves out of white eyelet and laced blue ribbons through. It was a lot of hard work but I was pleased, as my husband was surprised.

Jerry has a lot of fun with Fern's son Jimmy, and with Kenneth and Louella. We had never heard of trick or treat 'til Jimmy moved next door and on Halloween we learned also what a "tick-tack" was.

The summer was soon gone and after all my hard work of redoing the upstairs, Elmer decided to move to Markle to be closer to his work and the lumber yard. This pleased me for it was going home to me, and we would be halfway between his parents and mine. Harry Y. found a house for us close to the time I was due at the hospital.

All arrangements had been made for Jerry and Linda to stay with Grandpa and Grandma Mossburg, the bottom drawer was full of baby clothes again, and two names had been chosen. As usual Elmer put the "whammy" to the name I had chosen for a boy. I had decided to name him "Daniel Elmer." Elmer hated the name Daniel and turned thumbs down, so I gave Jerry the choice between Kim, Todd, or Kirby and he chose Kirby. My mother said she would like for us to use Dennis for one of the names. A little girl was to be Judith Elaine. Everybody was pleased with the girl's name.

On the morning of the 22nd of September we knew the time had come.

I had no qualms this time about leaving my little ones because they would rather stay with Grandpa and Grandma than they would at home. I knew I would have to overhaul them when I got home because they would be spoiled rotten, but was so thankful for the love showered on both of them.

I had wanted so much to see the house we were going to move into before I went to the hospital so Elmer said we could go early and stop at Pete's to eat before we went to the hospital. The house left a lot to be desired but it would give me lots to think about while I was in the hospital. We had just started to enjoy our chicken dinner at Pete's when a pain nearly knocked me off my chair! Elmer asked what was the matter and I said we had better go! "And leave all this chicken?" he asked. I felt like if we stayed he might have more to regret than the loss of his chicken by leaving! We tore to the hospital and the closer we came to it the better I felt. It was a lazy Sunday afternoon and there weren't any patients in our end of the place. We were old hands at the business by now—when Elmer asked if I cared if he sat in the car and listened to the ball game, I told him to go ahead. He came in to check on my progress every now and then, and when 3:00 came he said, "I would have had time to eat three chicken dinners!"

The tempo picked up around 4:00 and at a little after 8:00 we had our second son! He weighed over eight pounds. And what I remember most at first sight of him were his sweet little hands. They were so chubby with a row of dimples across each tiny fist.

Dr. Meade said, "This boy sure spoiled your street fair, didn't he?" The Bluffton Street Fair started on Tuesday and I could listen to the whole thing. I was very happy to be where I was with a new baby to love and watch grow.

Before Kirby was born Jerry started school. My heart ached to think of him going but knew it had to be. The bus forgot to stop for him and he ran out the door after it and didn't have time to say "goodbye." I can still see him running as fast as his legs would carry him across the railroad so he could get on the bus with Kenny and Louella.

As I lay in the hospital I thought of so many things, one of them being how thankful I was for three strong, healthy babies. The responsibility seemed awesome and I prayed for good health and guidance in raising them. I could not deny that our lives had changed considerably since Elmer had gone to Fort Wayne to work. He was gone in the mornings before the kids got up and many times didn't get home until after they were in bed. On weekends he was too worn out to give them any attention. This worried me considerably and I was ready to chuck the whole thing and go back to the way we were. He had become too deeply involved to turn back, so there was no other way to go except full speed ahead.

We did meet many very fine people and made friendships that lasted for years. Among them were Ward and Alma who came to Buckeye to talk to Elmer about a house. Linda wore a little short navy blue white polka dotted dress and her little feet were bare that day when she ran into the room where they were. They both made a grab for our little curly head and asked what her name was. With her big eyes shining, she replied, "My name is 'Linda', but everybody calls me 'Honey'!" As long as we knew them they never forgot about "Honey."

The day finally came when Kirby Dennis and I went home. The two were glad to see him. Jerry wanted to hold him and Linda wanted to feed him. I really had more help than I knew what to do with.

We got so involved with plans for our move that the poor baby almost got lost in the shuffle. He was a very contented baby and I had time to spend with the other two who kept me busy.

In October we moved. All the fellows who worked with Elmer loaded our stuff on the Lumber Yard truck and moved us to Markle before you could say "Jack Robinson." All I did was sit by the door and direct traffic. Anna Boxell, who had stayed with us after the baby was born, made beds and helped with all the other things that needed doing. Fern had kept Kirby, Grandma Mossburg had Linda and Jerry got off the school bus at Carl and Mary's. That night we collected our family and settled down for the night in our home in Markle.

We were back to paying rent—a thing we said we would never do again. Rent was a lot higher than it had been. We were now paying twelve dollars a month, which was twice what we paid when we were first married. We now enjoyed water in the house and our first bathroom, so maybe it was worth it. We had a nice big front porch where the kids could play. Jerry went to his new school with Joan and Emma Jean. I got acquainted with my new neighbor Alberta and liked her very much, but I sadly missed Buckeye and all the good friends and neighbors we left behind. I missed Elmer's folks, Grace, Howard and Aunt Em. I saw them nearly every day and missed them so very much.

When Christmas came we had the families on both sides of the house spent the day with us. It was a real hot day and we opened the doors and windows to let the breeze in. The two kept saying, "when is it going to snow?"—but it was a long way from snowing that day!

After a good turkey dinner, we opened our gifts. The fellows at the elevator sent gifts to Jerry and Linda! It was nice to know they missed us rather than being glad we were gone.

I know Elmer's parents missed the children and I sometimes felt guilty that we made the move. However, I did see much more of my husband. We had a date every Tuesday night. No matter how busy he was, he was home by 8:00 p.m. and we spent the evening together listening to Fibber McGee and Molly, over a bottle of Pepsi and a maple Wayne Bun. This was the night set aside to talk. I spent a lot of time cooped up with the three little ones and dying to enjoy a little adult conversation.

I know he didn't understand my needs any more than I could understand his giving his whole life to his work. On Tuesday nights we had time to talk these things over, and in time these problems were worked out. He was not only dedicated to his work but also to the fact that five people depended on him for their needs and he was determined his children would have a better life than he had had. His mother was the mainstay in their family. His father was a kind and loving person but a very poor manager and Elmer and Howard had a hard time growing up.

Kirby was my companion on many long winter evenings. The other two children were in bed by 8:00 p.m., and I held my little boy and rocked him. That old rocker had a lot of miles on it.

On October 25th, Elmer had to register for the draft and an uneasiness dogged my footsteps.

1941

This is our first Christmas without Grandma Moss-burg and oh, how we miss her. She died January 17th, almost a whole year ago. Grandpa moved to town near us. I know he is not happy but is doing the best he can to make the best of it. He loves the kids so much that I know his tomorrows will all be brighter because of them. They love their Grandpa too and are always glad to see him. He and Grace hurried down here Christmas morning to watch the kids get up and make their discoveries under the Christmas tree. They had a wonderful time but I know that deep down all we grownups had aching hearts. I know she was here, I could feel her nearness, but I have been so homesick for her that at times I think I can't go another day without talking to her. I loved her and I know that she loved me. She was one of the most unselfish and generous people I ever knew. I knew her for twelve years and never once did she ever find fault with me or anything I ever did, but was always on hand with help or praise, whichever I needed most. I shall never forget her comforting words before Kirby was born. I was down in the dumps, sick as a horse and feeling absolutely incapable of giving birth to and caring for another baby. We were making mincemeat that day when I told her about the new baby on the way. She stopped her grinder and looking me straight in the eye she said, "Well, it is a lucky baby to be born with you for its mother. I only wish I could know before I die that Grace and Howard were as happy and contented as Elmer is!" What a wonderful, wonderful thing to say and how wonderful of her to say it! Not that she was right, for I felt very humble and unworthy of her praise, but her wonderful faith in me gave me inspiration to be a better mother and wife. I vowed that day that if or whenever my sons should marry I would try to be the same kind of a mother to their wives as my mother-in-law was to me. I have recorded here this incident so if in years to come I shall forget, I will certainly be reminded when I browse through the Christmas diary. I know also that when we die it is only the part of us that we can see that really dies. The soul of us never dies but lives on in the good we have done to others. So shall Elmer's mother live on in me and I shall try to make the lives of my children rich as mine has been for having known her.

Our tree was a beautiful little tree and the children loved it. Grace and Grandpa ate breakfast with us. We spent the day with Mom and Dad. This has been a "muff" Christmas for Linda Gay. Grandma and Grandpa Dennis Santa left one there for her, Aunt Grace brought her one and Gretchen and Harry met Old Santa somewhere and he gave them one for her. Jerry thinks Santa should know better than to bring one little girl three muffs and three dolls all at once!

1942

This Christmas we are spending in our own home. We love it here but worked liked beavers before we moved in. Our living room is a big one and our furniture looked lost when we first moved in. There is a space of three lots where our little Indians can run. I know we are going to be very happy here. We sold our place in Buckeye for $800 and paid $2,000 for this one but we've got out of debt before so I guess we can do it again. It is worth being in debt to be off that busy street with the children.

Grace, Howard and Aunt Em stayed all night Christmas Eve. Grandpa Mossburg lives in his little trailer in our garden and came up early. Our beds were sort of crowded but we had a good time and besides, who can sleep on Christmas Eve? Elmer and I tore down the back stairway at the peep of dawn because the three were astir early. I can never sleep for fear I will miss their waking up. They always call out to each other in loud whispers and hold a conference before they slip out of bed and creep down the stairs. I love to hear them and thank God that there is always something for them under the tree. I can remember so well one Christmas when

I was a child there was no money for Santa Claus. We had been told over and over but I would not believe it until the morning when there was nothing for us. I tried not to cry but my heart ached nearly to the point of bursting. Badly as I felt, I know now my parents must have felt worse. Too much stress on gifts, you say? No, I don't think so. Children learn when they are very young to look to their parents for all good things that make them happy and secure. Later they learn to look to God, the parent of us all, for security and happiness, and that the packages under the tree are a symbol of our love. To me gift giving is a physical proof of spiritual love. When we come to the place where we have nothing to give to our children, our fellow man and our God, we have come to a pretty sad state indeed.

After a good breakfast we left Aunt Em, Grace, Howard and Grandpa to spend the day together and we bundled up the three in the car and spent the day with Mom and Dad and the girls. Dad and Mom still have Mary and Marjorie to keep their Christmas young. We had a very nice day and tucked three tired, happy little people into bed on Christmas night. May I never forget to be thankful for such a wonderful time as Christmas!

1943

think I shall always remember this Christmas as being one of the happiest I have ever known! For a little while, the war was shut out except for the kahike candle, which we lit as a reminder that Mary's new friend was spending Christmas in Italy with the army. Howard didn't get home Christmas Eve but came the next day. Grace watched supper for me while the children and I went to Fort Wayne to get Dorothy and Darwin so they could spend Christmas Eve with us. It was a beautiful evening. Grandparents Dennis, Mary, Marjorie and her friend Cloyd Grover were here too. Before supper Jerry read a scripture and we sang Christmas songs. I'll never forget the feeling of reverence and love that came over me as our son, aged nine, read from his Bible that he had earned by selling pictures. I'll never forget Linda and little Kirby both sitting on Grandpa Mossburg's lap singing "Silent Night" as loud as anyone. I'll not soon forget the candlelight reflections on the faces of all these so dear to me. I'm so grateful that we are all together once more and in good health. Of course Grandma Mossburg is gone, but somehow I feel that she enjoyed our Christmas too. I'll never forget our beautiful big tree loaded with gifts. The children's eyes sparkled with anticipation and they could hardly eat supper, they were so excited! After the fun was over we washed dishes. We took Dorothy and Darwin home but the three were having too much fun to go along, so they stayed home with Grandpa. Howard came the next day and helped us eat the scraps. That night we all went to Aunt Em's house.

1944

On February 2nd, Elmer went to Indianapolis to get his physical. I was worried sick and didn't know what to do. He didn't pass so I had something to worry about anyway. His health.

Our Christmas should have been a very happy one but the clouds of war dulled the bright cheerfulness and a heavy uneasiness hung over us. We spent Sunday with Mom and Dad. We were all there for which I was very thankful. It was a beautiful Christmas. The snow was deep. Grace came home on Sunday and Howard early Christmas morning. Aunt Em was here and Grandpa. We were up a little after 5:00 a.m., because we heard feet hit the floor in the children's room. Linda was a sleepy head, though, and had to be awakened. Elmer lighted the candles and we sat yawning in our nightclothes because we had no ambition to dress. We waited for Howard before we opened our gifts, after which we had breakfast. In the afternoon Howard took the boys out to play in the snow. Grace and Grandpa stayed with the three while we took Howard to Fort Wayne. We spent the evening with Ward and Alma. Alma and I walked to Earl and Esther's. It was the most beautiful night I think

I have ever seen. The snow was crisp and the air was cold. The moon was so bright that I could read the time on my new wristwatch. There is a sad story connected with this watch. I unknowingly bamboozled myself out of one with diamonds in it. It was the same old tale. Since the children were growing I was feeling mighty crowded in my tiny kitchen. Now, there was a partition between it and our tiny dining room, so one day I hunted up Grandpa's old wrecking bar and started in. I was getting along fine until I discovered the house was getting cold as a barn and found the thermostat lying all battered in a pile of plastering I had beaten off the wall from the kitchen side! I gulped in surprise and tried unsuccessfully to swallow the lump that came in my throat. I knew that I'd better do something quickly. I saw Hoover's truck over at Jack's so lost no time in getting over there. I know they both thought I was nuts. They looked at each other and started laughing but I couldn't find anything funny to laugh about. If I had known a few words of magic I would certainly have made use of them to restore that wall to its former condition! They soon had the thermostat replaced on the living room wall and I had the consolation of knowing my little four-year-old Kirby wouldn't freeze to death. The next thing was to do something with all the electric wire hanging down from the ceiling, but what do you do with electric wires that hang down from the ceiling? They won't come loose even when you swing on them. I tried that, so I called Agnes and told her what a mess I had gotten myself into and for her to ask Paul how to disconnect the wires. He said to tell me they'd be right over and to leave the wires alone before I electrocuted myself. While Paul worked on the wiring, Agnes helped me haul out the plastering and clean up the mess. By 4:00 we were done except for the plastering to be done and the linoleum to be bought and installed. I begged them to stay for supper but they said they just couldn't bear to be around to see me get shot, so away they went! When the kids came home from school Jerry said, "Gee whiz, Mom, won't Daddy be mad?" When they heard him drive in at 6:00, they retired to the living room and peeped around the corner. I guess they felt safer there. Only Grandpa stood beside me in my hour of need! When Elmer came in he took one look and got the strangest look on his face, but never said a word! I waited and waited for the hour of reckoning but it never came—just a slow torture gnawed at my insides. I did the painting and papering, but the worst thing was the floor and I couldn't do that. It was my turn to entertain my Sunday school class and I just didn't know what in the world I was going to do. He let me sweat it out 'til four days before the party and said, "You'd better be getting that linoleum if you want it laid before your party!" I went into action at once and the night of the party instead of my house smelling sweet, the rancid odor of linoleum paste permeated the air. To me it smelled of accomplishment, of something over and done with and I do mean, "done with." I took an oath on a rusty crow bar that never again would I tear out a partition! Now, since Christmas is over, my husband has confided in me that he didn't like being all cramped up in that little kitchen either but what irked him most was that he had saved money to buy me a really nice watch and had to spend it for linoleum!

1945

This is the first Christmas Raymond has spent with us but my brand new brother-in-law spent the day in Japan. Darwin spent Christmas on his new job and Dorothy came to our house. Grace came home and together we prepared Christmas feast. Howard didn't get to come because the bus didn't run. The roads were a solid glare of ice and we hardly expected our company to come but with Raymond at the wheel they came sliding in safely. We had a good turkey dinner after which we opened our gifts. The fun broke up early because of the weather. Elmer, Grace and I took Dorothy home and Grandpa stayed with the three. He has as much fun with their toys as they do. We read the book *Taps for Private Tussy* this week. Grace acquired the name of "Aunt Vittie" and Elmer is "Uncle Mott." Jerry's papers were late getting in Christmas Eve, so Elmer and I donned our warm clothes and helped him on his paper route and what fun we had. It was almost impossible to stand up, it was so icy. It was a beautiful night, the trees were splendid in their diamonds. They moaned from their ice-encrusted joints when the wind stirred them a little. Many limbs came tumbling to the ground under the weight of their icy coats, sending splinters of crystal across the glassy highway. My toes and fingers nearly froze but I never felt more alive and certainly never happier. Everyone on his route was so kind. Jerry received many nice gifts. We were done at last and hurried home to our warm house where we devoured hot ham sandwiches.

1946

A long time ago when God threw Adam and Eve out of the Garden of Eden, he ordered them to earn their living by the sweat of their brows. I always believed it would be a lot easier to grow up knowing how to work than to have the necessity of it dumped on one all at once.

There is no reason work can't be enjoyable. My mother had a plan that took the sting out of the word and actually made it seem like play. She made out little slips of paper with a chore to be done one each of them. Then we could do what was on our own slip or trade. The work seemed to go twice as fast and I could grab my book and take off for my favorite reading place.

My mother's thinking was that if you grew up and married a rich man you were lucky but if you married a poor man you already knew how to work.

My feelings on the subject are that learning to work teaches responsibility and, rich or poor, we all have responsibilities.

Tomatoes had become a farm crop in Indiana and the kids and I had helped several farmers set tomatoes. I packed a hardy lunch and we were up and out early. Linda earned her first watch setting tomatoes. What the kids earned was theirs to spend as they pleased. If their money was spent for something foolish, it was their loss and they knew better next time. I usually set with Kirby because he wasn't very old and needed help once in a while.

This spring I had promised Jerry I would set with him. There were four setters to a planter and Colleen and Phyllis were the other two.

Before time came for the job to be started, I received a message from the Stork and he said I had better not set tomatoes! Jerry didn't get to work very long because he came down with the mumps. Of course it wasn't long before Linda and Kirby had them too.

Early in the spring we had bought baby chicks to raise in the place we prepared in the top of our barn. In May they were ready to dress and sell. Elmer stayed home and helped me and we dressed seventy fryers. I happened to go out to the garden and noticed the strawberries were ready to pick. You don't argue with a ripe strawberry, so I started picking. This was solely my job because Elmer is color-blind and picks as many green ones as ripe ones. I picked thirty quart and when I finished it was time to deliver papers for Jerry. Elmer couldn't do it because he was not familiar with the route, and all three kids were sick and couldn't go along to direct him. We couldn't both go and leave three sick children on their own, so the only solution was for me to go. Elmer stayed home, weighed and wrapped the chickens and I started out delivering papers, strawberries and chickens. It was 10:00 p.m. when I got done, and that day had to be the biggest workday I had ever lived through.

Before the children were fully recovered I came down with the mumps! I was terribly sick and Elmer called Dr. Meade. When he came in Jerry had just taken a batch of bread out of the oven that Elmer had set to raise the night before. He couldn't believe his eyes and wondered how old the kids were. He said, "You don't see much of that these days. People have forgotten to teach their kids how to work or think it's a disgrace or something." I was ordered to stay down 'til the swelling was gone, and our three little ones took care of their mother the best they knew how. I was worried about the affects of mumps on my baby but Dr. Meade said, "You needn't worry about that. All that will happen is that the baby will be immune and never have the mumps."

On May 30th I wrapped up in a blanket and went out and sat in the swing. I could hear the band playing as the residents of our town marched to the cemetery. Jerry marched as a proud Boy Scout.

I learned to knit this year and knit Jerry a sweater for Christmas, a scarf and cap for Kirby, white, pink and blue three-piece sweater sets for our new baby and crocheted a white lace dress for Linda. The kids were excited, and nobody thought anything else than the baby would be a little girl. I secretly hoped so, too, for then we would have two of each, which I thought would be an ideal family. Linda had already named her little sister and the baby was Mary Lou.

Linda and Kirby have lots of fun together. They like to play "dress up" and he is just as fine a lady in his high-heeled shoes as she is. When Linda started school he hardly knew what to do with himself all day but about 3:30, he dressed up in his long dress and high heels and waited for her at Tedford's corner. This year he started to school, too, and three hungry children crash the door at noon starved to death. Their favorite lunch is peanut-butter sandwiches, canned peaches and hot chocolate. I am so busy but so happy!

The most terrible thing happened in October. Our dear little friend Agatha took her own life! I will never forget her. The last time we were together we had so much fun. She had been ill in her mind and we all thought she was recovering. Poor little Billy is at the age where he needs her most.

Our friends, Paul and Alice gave the kids a puppy. It is a Pekingese and cute as it can be. The kids named it "Lucky."

In July we bought a cottage at North Webster and have been remodeling it.

In November Elmer was initiated into the Masonic Lodge. Ward and Alma, George and Vera, Paul and Alice, Friz and Eleanor and Billy and her husband came from Fort Wayne. The fellows accompanied Elmer to help him through his big evening and the girls stayed with me. They surprised me with a shower for our baby soon to be born. We had a good time and when the men came home we had pie and coffee, and a lot of good conversation. After they were gone we talked far into the night of how wonderful it is to have such good friends. It makes his having gone to work in Fort Wayne almost worthwhile! These were all people he had met through his work.

When December came I did my shopping in the early part because Dr. Meade had my time set around the 20th, and I had to have everything ready for the holidays for three children would feel bad enough without their mom at Christmas. I could not vision the trio beating down the stairs and not finding something on the tree for them.

They were in the church Christmas program and Linda needed a new dress. On December 6th I lined the baby basket for the fourth time and in the afternoon started on Linda's dress. It was a tiresome job as it was hard to lean over and treadle the sewing machine at the same time. I guess the resident of my insides thought someone was knocking at his door and decided to determine who it was, because next morning I woke up with the familiar signal to get going. The house was a mess, Linda's dress was only half done and Elmer had concrete to pour for Ward and Alma. He was on his way to the truck to go to Fort Wayne when I called him.

He said, "Can't you wait 'til I get that concrete poured?" I think that guy has a hang-up and thinks that, if he can just keep on eating his chicken or pouring concrete, by some miracle when he raises his head, it will all be over!

Mary Lou was growing more insistent by the minute, so Elmer called Paul and Agnes. It is certainly good to have friends you can depend on. We had helped each other often and felt free to ask them. They came hurrying over just like we hurried to their house once when Agnes called for help when Paul removed a supporting beam and the garage roof fell in! Paul went to pour concrete and Agnes was stuck with three kids and a dirty house. My neighbor, Ruby, to whom I shall always be grateful, finished Linda's dress. I had planned to make cookies and fill the larder before I went to the hospital but this little soul took me by surprise because I thought I had at least two weeks to go. We finally got going, and the long painful hours dragged on until 3:30. Our fourth child, a dear little red-headed boy, upset the apple cart. The count was three and one instead of two and two. My first thought was of Linda—how she would miss her Mary Lou!

For some time I had a secret hidden away in my heart. I knew that as busy as Elmer had been, he would never have had time to think of a name for a boy—so, I decided to say nothing about it 'til the doctor came asking for his name. Then I was going to name him Daniel Elmer and it would be too late for him to object. Before he left the hospital, he stuck his finger down on my nose and said, "Now, before I leave here I want something made perfectly clear. That boy is *not* going to be Daniel Elmer!" Well, there went Daniel Elmer again!

We can always remember the day Markle was in the Roto section of the *News-Sentinel*. It was the day Jim was born and Jerry had sold over 140 papers in advance. When Elmer got home, Agnes was having an awful time. The wind had scattered papers all over the yard and she, with the kids, was trying to recover them. All the kids in the neighborhood came running when Elmer drove in and when he told them it was a boy, it nearly broke Linda's heart. Janet cried, too, because Linda cried. Linda said, "Well, I'm not going to help take care of that little brat!"

I was trying to think of just the right name to fit this sweet little son and came up with "Patrick Shane." That was it! It just fit him! When Elmer came the next day he was all excited because HE had thought of just the right name! Our baby was born on the 7th anniversary of Pearl Harbor. Two of our town boys had lost their lives in the war and he had gone to their parents and ask if we might name our son after them. They were pleased and so our little boy was named "James Harold." "Patrick Shane" slid into oblivion! I had borne four babies and didn't get to name any of them! Just for that I wouldn't have any more!

Before the baby was born my Mom said, "Now, why don't you try to have a dark-haired one this time?" So, before they saw him up close for the first time, I painted his little curl with mascara! My mom was pleased, but when I washed it off and that one little red curl showed up, she gave up and said she guessed she'd just have to wait for one of my sisters to go into action!

I was thankful to be home for Christmas. Mr. and Mrs. Winters went to California and brought Grace home to stay with us. They couldn't have chosen a better time to go. She cooked and did the washing for us. When my neighbor, Pauline, came to the hospital to see me, she said she waited 'til she thought the house might need cleaning but when she went over it looked better than it did when I was at home! Elmer had a system that worked, but I'm sure that after he had been at the helm as long as I had they wouldn't pay any more attention to him than they did to me.

Christmas morning the kids were up bright and early as usual on this great day. Kirby had a hard time getting settled for the night. About 9:30 Santa Claus awakened him and he couldn't get back to sleep. Jack Adams brought him over and we never did find out who was under the whiskers. Next morning Kirby said, "Mama I dreamed I saw Santa Claus and he was standing right by my bed!" Jerry said, "No, you didn't dream it because I saw him too!" I think for a while Jerry mistrusted his belief that there is no Santa Claus!

Another wonderful year is about to end. We love our little family and I wouldn't trade places with anybody in the world!

1947

*T*his has been a nice Christmas except the explorers have decreased considerably.

Grace and Wayne were married in January and Grace is spending her Christmas in the hospital with their baby son, Paul Wayne. It seems so strange to get used to her being married. She has been at home so long. I am so glad she has a home and a family of her own. She loved the kids so much and I am glad she can have children of her own, to love and care for.

Marjorie and Cloyd have a baby girl, Cathy Marie. Little Jim will have some cousins to play with. Mary is married and living in Memphis. They were married September 12th last year. They didn't get home for Christmas this year. It was Mary's first Christmas away from home and we all miss her. We called her Christmas Eve.

Dorothy is with Darwin on a new job and they didn't get home either.

Marjorie and her family and I with my family spent Christmas Eve with Mom and Dad. Mom had a nice supper after which we opened our gifts. We girls had pooled our money and bought groceries for the folks for Christmas. They were really surprised and so appreciative of our gift.

We came home early and the kids were soon in bed but we could hear them whispering for a long time before they went to sleep.

The boys rolled Elmer out about 5:30 to go on the paper route. They worked up such an appetite that we ate breakfast before the explorers set out to discover what was under the Christmas tree. Everyone was happy with what they found but no one more so than I. Santa had brought me a set of fireplace fixtures so I know that someday the dream of my life will be realized—that of knitting in front of my fireplace! Elmer's cousin Cara sent me a book of the complete poem of "Hiawatha." I shall treasure it forever!

In the afternoon Elmer, Lucky and I took a long walk down the county line and down 224 to 116 then back home again. How wonderful to have eyes to see, ears to hear, and legs to walk on. I hope I never forget how blessed our family has been.

I was initiated into Eastern Star in April.

1948

This Christmas Jim and Cathy chased each other in their walker and scooter. Paul sat on his daddy's lap and watched.

We had a buffet supper and ate in the living room around the tree. It was a very pretty tree this year. The Murphys and the Curtises were absent, but will enjoy the season in their part of the world, I am sure.

Dad gave Mom a wedding ring, which is the first one she ever had. She is so proud of it.

The very nicest gift I received was a note from my husband saying that he had paid off our debt at the bank and we are the proud owners of a checking account! Out of debt at last—what a wonderful feeling!

It was so nice to have our family with us for this lovely season. Grandpa Mossburg enjoys the kids so much!

We spent Christmas day at home playing our new record player.

I always take a good look at my blessings at this time of year and have found that the more of us there are to love, the greater the capacity of my love. It is so nice to have babies around the tree once more. We hope that as time goes on lots more will gather around. It is with a sad heart that I remind myself that we won't always be adding and that someday a lesser number will gather around the Christmas tree.

1949

All has gone well with us this year. We have enjoyed a prosperous summer and were able to buy a beautiful new carpet to replace the one with the big hole right in the middle that we had to keep covered with a throw rug. After our carpet was installed it was impossible to open the front door. Being married to a carpenter isn't always easy. Everyone seems to think if you need anything nailed on or sawed off it is a cinch—that it will be done right away, because the guy with the saw and hammer lives right here! This assumption couldn't be farther from the truth. I waited and waited for him to cut that door off and when I got tired of yelling through the hardwood to whomever might be on the other side that they must come to the side door, I ripped the thing off its hinges and with Jerry's help dragged it down to the basement workshop. We ran it through the saw and rehung it but it was a wee bit long on one side, so off it came and down to the basement and through the saw it went again. This time, daylight filtered under the door on one side but it dragged the carpet on the other. I made sure this time it was short enough and when we hung it the third time, it cleared the carpet with about an inch to spare! I called my neighbor, Evelyn, to come over and to walk right in the front door! When she came in she admired our work but said, "I don't know why I opened the door when I could have just crawled under it!"

For a long time, I had a desire to put out a big strawberry patch. This spring I set out several hundred plants in the lots back of Jack's garage. We went all out and paid over $600 for a tiller to take care of them. The thing was so big and clumsy it would have sprained the muscles of Charles Atlas to operate it. It was just too much for a fifteen-year-old boy and a forty-year-old woman and we had to call for help. Needing to be three or four other places, it didn't set too well that Elmer had to waste his time at home. (I don't mention this incident often, but it was just too funny to omit.) Elmer was plowing away when something went wrong with one of the tines and he needed to remove it. He worked and worked but was unable to remove the things and his temperature was getting higher by the minute. I moved in and said, "I don't know why that thing is so hard to get off. Mr. Tullis just went like this—" and when I said "like this," the thing fell off in my hand! Jerry ran over to the edge of the patch and sat down to laugh, but I cackled right there in front of him with that tine still in my hand! He wasn't very happy at first but finally had a good laugh too. Next year I hope to be Markle's Strawberry Queen but I don't think Elmer cares to be the King! If they do well we should be up to our necks in strawberries.

We spent our Christmas Eve with Marjorie and Cloyd and Cathy. Mary came to our house and went with us, but went home with Mom and Dad.

We didn't stay long because "baby" Grover was due and "Mama" was tired out.

After the kids were in bed Elmer and I slipped downstairs to put the electric train together. We had so much fun we almost forgot to go to bed.

Next morning we were up early and after church we started preparing supper. Fern had bought a turkey but since she was working she didn't have time to prepare it so brought it over to me.

We had a good supper and lots of fun. Jim Daley brought two of his boy friends and their three girl friends. Linda gazed in awe at the girls all evening and after they were gone she said, "Gee, Mom, I wish I was old enough to be Jim's girl!"

When the festivities were over, I was dead tired from such a full week. On Monday the 19th, I had been initiated into Psi Iotz Xi and enjoyed it very much. I am an assistant leader of the Girl Scouts and we went caroling on Friday night. I enjoy scouting very much; Linda and I leave the "men" at home and have our nights out. We have enjoyed lots of cookouts and camping out at the "Mamie Sunley" cabin in the woods over by Huntington. They have a very good leader, Lesta Fox. She is a lot of fun to be with, and when we took the girls to Detroit, Hazel Brunson, Glenna Stookey, the other two assistants, Lesta and I had as much fun as the girls.

The lovely Christmas season is almost over once more and a new year will soon be knocking at our door. I won't have to tell it to "go around to the side" because it can come right in the front. (Elmer put a higher threshold under the door to keep the snow out.)

1950

I will have to concede defeat as far as my berry patch is concerned. It was too much for me. The weather didn't cooperate either. It was a dry spring and nothing grew except the weeds. I must confess that when I dreamed of a berry patch all I pictured were bowls of luscious berries. I forgot to take into account the hours of hoeing and weeding I had neither the time nor the strength for. The patch was a disgrace to anyone who considered herself a gardener as I did. I didn't harvest enough berries to even pay for the gas for "Old Tiller."

I had thought it would be a good thing for Linda and Kirby to help with and I would share the profits, which would teach them the "reward of patient industry." When the few berries that survived the heat started to ripen, the two kids and I took off for the berry patch while Grandpa ran herd on Jim.

Kirby was the first one to be excused because he held every berry up for my inspection with the question, "Is this one ripe enough, Mom?" By that time it was already too late because he had picked it off.

Linda lasted three or four minutes longer and baited me by saying, "Mom, if you don't make me pick berries I will help

Grandpa watch Jim, do the ironing and get supper." I rose to the bait and she was true to her promise. She made half a dozen trips over to the patch to find out how to make noodles, which she wanted to put with the beef I had on cooking for supper.

That night she had a nice supper for a little girl her age, but her big brother, who felt a little superior because he had been working with his dad, surveyed the table and the dish of noodles. Turning to his dad he said, "Well, Dad, pass the two by fours!"

After the referee blew the whistle, we settled down to a good supper and the noodles were delicious, although they were a little wide.

Our Linda Gay had to start wearing glasses this summer. The doctor thought she wouldn't need to wear them after she got a little older. We hope not anyway. Kirby was quite intrigued with them and found a pair of Elmer's discarded frames and wore them at half-mast on his nose. One day he said, "Mom, I can see so much better with these on, why don't you get some glass put in them for me?"

Grandpa's trailer burned in November and he spent Christmas with Grace and her family. Paul now has a little sister, Mary Esther, to add joy to their Christmas.

Linda and Kirby came downstairs at 3:30 and we chased them back to bed. No sleep the rest of the night! About 5:30, after listening to them whisper for nearly two hours we crawled out and yawned around the Christmas tree.

It beats me how kids can be so everlastingly sleepy when it's time to go to school, but can lie awake half of Christmas Eve and be bright as a new dollar at 5:00 a.m. the next morning! I guess that is a mystery that will never be answered.

I shall not soon forget this Christmas. I was presented with a little notebook with instructions that led me all over the house. At each designated place I found a number of dollar bills. Jerry and Kirby followed carrying a pillowcase into which I was to deposit the money. At the end of the tour the last note in the notebook said that if one cent of it was spent on the kids he would take the whole thing away from me! When I counted the money I had $100!

Old Santa Claus was very good to all the kids this year. He brought Kirby and Jim black cowboy outfits. When we got ready to go to Mom and Dad's, Jim said, "Grandma won't know who I are will her. Her will fink I are a cowboy!" Dear little Jim! They both looked so cute in their outfits and wanted to wear them every day.

We came home in a blinding snowstorm and are happy to be in our own cozy nest. Jerry and Duff went skating, Kirby, Linda and Emma Jean went for a walk and tired little Jim went to bed. Daddy and Mother took a nap and then listened to the new records.

So ends another Merry Christmas and we pray for a New Year when all people will join hands in *"Peace on Earth."*

As soon as possible I went to town and had myself a ball. I had never had so much money just for myself before! I had been instructed to spend every red cent! I bought a beautiful tan suit and to go with it a brown tweed wool coat, a brown hat with a turned up brim, a good pair of "Air-step" shoes, a purse, and gloves. I found I had money left over so I bought a beautiful blouse to go with my new suit. (In this year of 1980, it costs almost what my pillowcase turned out to buy the gas to go to town. Ah! For the good old days!)

1951

Our Jerry is a senior this year. I can't believe how fast the years have gone! It seems only yesterday I sent him off to school with a heavy heart that my little boy was growing up too fast. Kirby wasn't even born yet and Linda was just a little two-year-old girl. That summer she shared my lap with Kirby and could sing, "South of the Border" all the way through. We all sang a lot in those days. It was a good way to keep the two little ones occupied while we were driving. Elmer had a guitar and we sang. That was before the beginning of his career in Fort Wayne. Much earlier, when life had less responsibilities, he belonged to a little group that got together and played and sang. Dean Boxell and Elmer played guitar, Carl Sparks mandolin, Billy Woods and Carl Brinniman violins, Wayne Dolby banjo and Lew Dolby the bones.

One time when we still lived in Buckeye, Carl Hunnicut went to Chicago to get a piano some friend told him he could have if he would come after it. Another party had one to get rid of so he brought us one too. It was a player piano and weighed about a ton but had a beautiful tone. One of the rolls that came with it was called "Falling Waters" and it was Jerry's favorite song. He was too little to reach the peddles while sitting so he hung on to the edge of the keyboard and peddled until his legs gave out and then ran out to play. It took him about all day to get through the song once.

That old piano was part of our family until we remodeled the house years later. Linda took piano lessons and stuck with it without any pressure from Mom, but Kirby's musical career was short-lived. There were too many things to do and too many kids to do them with for him to concentrate very long on his lesson. One day after I had nearly had to tie him to the piano bench, I heard strange sounds coming from the instrument. When I investigated, there he sat with his cowboy hat on, his holster around his waist, and with tears streaming down his face he was practicing his lesson with his water pistol! Oh, how I yearned for a place in the country where there were not so many distractions! We had been looking for a place for a long time but never seemed to be able to afford what was for sale.

We had a lovely white Christmas this year. We spent Christmas Eve with Mom and Dad. After we came home three tired kids went to bed. Jerry and two of his friends came back to the house before the three were asleep so they crawled out and came downstairs. We took pictures around the tree and the artificial fireplace on the east wall. After they were gone Elmer and I put the presents under the tree and headed for bed, for from past experiences we had a short night ahead of us. Before we got to sleep Jerry came home and made so much noise playing with the toy filling station that I had to get up and chase him off to bed.

Kirby and Jim came pounding down the stairs at 5:30 and it seemed I had hardly closed my eyes. We were soon out of bed to get an early start on the loveliest day of the year. We turned on the lights of the tree and on the little artificial fireplace. Jim was so excited he shook 'til he could hardly open his presents, while Linda tore into her package and found her long-wished-for skates. Kirby and Jim were so happy with toy filling station and freight stations.

Claude, Virginia, Sharon and Sandy Michaels came in the afternoon and were with us for supper. Virginia plays the piano beautifully and we sang carols. We also let loose on the "Whiffen-poor" song.

When the house was quiet and the family all bedded down for the night except me, I sat for a long time reviewing the events of the year, wondering how I could improve my own life. It seems like I am often too hard on the kids, I take on too many projects at one time, and too often I bark at my husband. I often feel so inadequate in this calling of mine. When I surveyed this job twenty-one years ago, the picture I came up with was a family of our kids (two girls and two boys) with a mother who always enjoyed getting a beautiful meal on the table on time, who waved a magic wand and the house was always immaculate, who always met her husband at the door with a clean dress on and smelling like a rose, who never raised her voice to her children who always responded to her kind requests. I try to remember that growing up isn't easy either, so this Christmas night I offered up a selfish prayer, "Make a better wife and mother out of me, Lord, give me patience, courage, wisdom and understanding. Care for my children and help them grow into good men and women with the help I am able to give them. Help me understand my husband better and help him remain true to his high ideals. If You can see fit to do this, Lord, life will be much sweeter for us and we won't be such a burden on You. Amen."

1952

This Christmas finds us in our home north of Markle. We had hunted a long time for a place in the country and once when I was visiting Mary Stahl on some O.E.S. business, I loved the way the sun shone in her big south window, and told her if they ever put their home up for sale we would like to have a chance to buy it. I had forgotten it for it had been so long ago. One day she called me and told me it was for sale but her husband, not knowing of her promise to me, had given first chance to someone else. Too bad for that person but good for us he was unable to finance the venture. Mary called again after we had sweated it out for a while. Elmer was working in the basement and told me to go look at it and if I liked it to tell her we would take it. I already knew I liked it, but was a little afraid of making that much of a commitment alone—because when we look at something, we often see two different things. Once we went to look at a place that was for sale and Elmer was interested in the structural part of the house while I took a tour of the flowerbeds and the trees. When I tore around the house to have him come see the beautiful lilac bushes he said, "For Heaven's sake, look at the

house! You're not going to be living in that lilac bush!" When I
went back to town with my report he said, "Did you tell her we
would take it?" Following my negative answer he commanded, "Go
call her up and tell her it is sold!" I was thrilled to pieces and could
hardly wait for moving day. At forty-one, I was pretty worn out
with chasing kids and capturing them long enough to come home
to eat and sleep, especially Jim who was always somewhere else!

The house was soon vacated but we had several things to do,
one of which was to sell our house in town. We planted a strawberry bed and moved our beloved shrubs and flowers to their new
home. Our garden was put in and crops planted and tended before
moving day finally arrived. Each time we went out we took a load
with us so when "M" day finally arrived it didn't take long to make
the move complete.

We were up early, had breakfast for the last time in the old home
and then started the final leg of our journey. Linda and I did the last-
minute cleaning and the four "men" started the hauling. I'll always
remember the red truck with the dollhouse on top of the pile and Jim
peeping out from underneath a table. Jerry and Kirby sat on top to
steady the load while Elmer herded the whole thing northward. The
old home was left with backward looks and sighs for the hill where
we slid in winter and for the beautiful evergreen tree that had sheltered us for so long, and for the fine neighbors we were leaving.

The hill was fine for sliding but I remember sometimes when
it wasn't any fun! We had to park the truck at the top of it and
Elmer had chased it twice when it started to roll. One day I was in
the back yard working in the flowers, and looking up, I saw the
thing starting down the hill and I wasn't sure Jim had gotten out
when I told him to. I was kicking up sod when I tore across the
yard to save him, but thank God, there he sat on the steps wrapped
up in his blanket! What a relief! The truck had to be pulled out of
the deep ditch and it had a muddy nose.

Once Kirby was sitting in the car and pushed on the clutch just enough to agitate gravity and if it hadn't hung up on a big rock, Jim and Grandpa, who were sitting in the lawn swing, would have had a big surprise! I can't say I was sorry to leave that hill.

The kids knew they were going to miss their playmates, but Jim missed Mrs. Crow, Mr. Brown and "the woman" (as he called Mrs. Brown). After a few days, he cried and wanted to go back home. Once when we visited Mary and Raymond in Memphis, we stopped at a gift shop and told the kids they could buy something for themselves. All Jim could find that he wanted was a sticker that said "Chattanooga" on it, for Mr. Brown's car! Mr. Brown was *so* pleased! He let Jim stick it on his windshield. After a few days Mrs. Brown told me that Emmet had teased Jim and made him angry. The next thing they knew, Jim was in the car scraping off his sticker!

We tumbled into bed that night tired but happy. Next day Linda left for church camp and Mama celebrated her birthday by rushing Jim to the hospital to get his head sewed up. He and Kirby and Mary Jane were playing in the shop and Jim fell and peeled his scalp back. It looked like the flap on an envelope! I froze to the spot but my resourceful friend Mildred grabbed clean dishtowels out of the drawer and slapped cold compresses on his head, yelling for me to call the doctor. I came out of my state of rigor mortis and went into action. Garl and Elmer came home just as we came in from the doctor. They went home and we took Jim to the hospital. Jim had fallen and hit his head on the corner of a metal toolbox.

Our summer, or what was left of it, was spent in our garden and kitchen preparing fortifications for the winter. Elmer worked on the job all day and spent half the night making our cellar ready to receive our beautiful jars of canned foods and mending the porch that led to it. Winter finds us well prepared. Our cellar is full, our oil tank is full and paid for, and we have three pigs and a hen house full of very accommodating hens.

Hens are such good companions! I love to sit in the hen house and talk to them. Often they cock their heads to one side and answer me and sometimes even argue in a ladylike manner. These are not too different from other "Hen Parties" I have attended, except when *these* girls disagree, instead of nit picking, they fly into each other with no holds barred and fight until one or the other of them has proved her point. They don't shake hands and hide their fury in the name of "Christian Fellowship," but sidle around to the far side of the building keeping a wary eye on the opponent. They remind me of a quotation from Shakespeare: "Beware of entrance to a quarrel, but being in, bear it, that the opposed may beware of thee."

This has been a busy year for Jerry. He graduated in May and since then has been working with his Dad and enjoying his new car. He is very proud of it and washes and polishes it 'til it's a wonder there is any paint left on it. He is a son to be proud of and if next year finds him in Uncle Sam's employ, I feel that the discipline he has had will be an asset to him in his new way of life. I feel that we will have some bad days ahead but will enjoy him while he is here and think about that time when it comes. His graduation party was the last big event in the old home.

Linda Gay had a nice summer—a vacation with Judy, a week at church camp and swimming at the quarry. Poor little girl—she is too young to be a grown up lady and too old to be a little girl! A change of schools has brought her new friends but she has not forgotten the old ones. Christmas Day brought a remodeled room for her and she is very proud of it. Her Daddy built a headboard, a desk and night tables for her room. Her Mom painted and did all the other necessary things to make her room nice. She spent most of the day there just sitting and looking.

Kirby-boy is fast growing up. He rated a new bicycle this year. He likes his new school and has made a lot of new friends. He spends a lot of time entertaining Grandpa who seems to be failing and doesn't get out as much as he used to. He reads a lot and tells the boys stories about when he was a boy. Jim's favorite one is about a dog that wasn't worth a dog-gone! Grandpa has told it so often that he is getting tired of it and tries to cut the story short. Jim always says, "No, now, Grandpa, that's not the way it was," and proceeds to tell the story without the abbreviation! This is Jim's last winter at home. Soon they will all be gone, leaving Grandpa, the dog and I to hold the fort all day.

We had a lovely little tree this first Christmas in our new home. It seems strange to be spending Christmas in this unfamiliar place but our familiar belongings surround us and the same faces smile around our table. Our supper was simple and after it was over we talked about other Christmases. Grandpa talked about Jerry's first Christmas and the little overalls he bought for him. I went upstairs and brought down my treasures and the little overalls were among them! Then we all laughed at how they measured on Jerry now. We looked over all the other things I have saved—the little shoes, the handmade dresses and an assortment of trinkets that is only junk to anyone except Elmer and me. We even have our letters we wrote to each other and they sound pretty silly now. I don't know why I save them!

After the dishes were done we gathered around the piano and sang. Grandpa usually stays in his room but this night he joined us and sang as loud as anybody.

Jerry brought his new girlfriend home, but she was a little bashful and didn't join in the singing—I think she was too young to realize that the louder you sing, the less you have to listen! We liked her very much and Jerry seems to be "head over heels." He was driving down the county line with the car windows open and she threw a snowball that sailed right past his nose. Of course, that was excuse enough to stop and talk, ending up with a date.

Strange things bring people together! If this turns out to be the real thing between him and Norma Jean, he can thank a snowball. His dad and mother were brought together by a door key. I had seen him at a party and he had been dating a friend, so he was not a complete stranger. I had been working at a restaurant and had a room in town because I got off work too late for Dad to come in after me. Elmer stopped in, and, on a dare from the brother of the girl he was dating, asked me to go for a ride. As usual, I couldn't make up my mind—but when I got to where I was staying, he sailed around the corner just as I was unlocking my door. He was very polite and asked if I needed any help, which, of course, I did. I gave him the key and he put it in his pocket and asked me to go for a ride with him. There was just nothing else to do since he had the key. It was a short ride, but it led to a long commitment, for that night he also took the key to my heart!

After our family was in bed, Elmer and I looked at all our greeting cards again. They are such an enjoyable part of Christmas!

A nice surprise came from the Lumber Yard. They sent us a big turkey and before we went to bed, we slid it into the oven. Next morning when the Christmas tree scouts came downstairs they didn't know whether to head for the tree or the turkey, it smelled so good.

We had to awaken Grandpa. I guess he was tired out from the fun of Christmas Eve. We enjoyed our gifts after our company came and then we enjoyed the turkey. Dorothy and Darwin surprised us because we didn't think they were coming. They all left early and we settled down to a quiet evening of reading.

This has been a beautiful year. The coming ones surely can't be any happier! Every Christmas I sum up the events of the year and say to myself, "This is it. This has to be the most beautiful year of my life!"

I hope we have given our children a good pattern to live by. I hope they feel this love that surrounds us and penetrates every fiber of our lives as I do. I hope it will inspire them to build good homes of their own and when we are gone, may they often return in memory and gather around the Christmas tree.

1953

*O*ur beloved Grandpa isn't with us any more. He died the day after Linda's fifteenth birthday. On her birthday, which was on Saturday, Elmer told me to take her to town and buy her presents and get out of the house for a while. Before I left I prepared Grandpa for the night and tried to feed him what the doctor had ordered, but he turned his head away because he was sick of soup and Jell-O. He had always been a big meat eater so I went to the kitchen and fixed some hamburger and crumbled it so he could eat it. He ate some of it and turned his head to look at me and said, "God will bless you, Alfreda!" Those were the last words he ever said. They will go with me down through the years and I know I will often be blessed as I have so often in the past! The next day he quietly slipped away. He rests in the Mossburg cemetery where the only Mossburg to come to this part of the country established his home many, many years ago.

Jerry and Norma Jean have become more than friends this summer. He knows that he can't make any plans because Uncle Sam is breathing down his neck! Finally, in October, he decided to enlist and get it over with, so he could get on with his life. I know there are dark days ahead; however many times in our deepest sorrow we find our greatest strength. I have written a few lines to sustain me in the days ahead.

> *In the secret chapel of my heart*
> *An altar's hidden there*
> *Secure from prying eyes and minds*
> *I lose myself in prayer.*
>
> *I have no certain time of day*
> *No man-made spot to kneel*
> *When I turn to God my wounded heart*
> *And ask His touch to heal.*
>
> *My world is tinged with sorrow now*
> *I try to hide my tears*
> *And hope they wash away the gloom*
> *That threatens coming years.*
>
> *When my darling is gone from me*
> *I'll countless times a day*
> *Camouflage him with my prayers*
> *From my secret hide-a-way.*

It is nearly time to write Christmas '54. Until now I haven't had the heart to finish our story for '53. The loss of Grandpa and the knowledge that Jerry would be leaving January 25, 1954, somehow dulled my enthusiasm for writing.

Christmas Day was a nice day. Jean stayed all night Christmas Eve and slept on Linda's mattress on the floor. Linda made herself a bed on the box springs. I guess necessity *is* the mother of invention!

We were up early as usual and opened our gifts after which we had a good breakfast. We all seem to like packages and more packages. Our tree is always loaded down even if we have to split a pair of socks and wrap them separately! Norma Jean seems to enjoy herself at our house with all the crazy goings-on. She and Jerry went to Fort Wayne to her sister's house and the Grovers, the Curtises and Dad and Mom spent the day with us.

Cathy, Dennis and Jim spent nearly the whole day on the floor in Grandpa's bedroom painting with Jim's watercolor set Santa brought him. They just about painted the whole bedroom floor. After Dorothy and Darwin left, Cathy said, "I'm sure glad that dog went home! You ought to see how he walked through our paints and smeared up the floor!"

We spent most of the day watching TV. This wonderful, wonderful thing happened to us in the early fall. We bought a used one from Clair Geiger and when he brought it we were lined up on the davenport like birds on a high-tension wire waiting for the miracle to happen. When he turned it on, *nothing* happened! He told Elmer later he couldn't bear the looks of disappointment on that many faces at one time, so he hurried to Zanesville and brought a new one for us to use until he could repair the other one.

Oh, the wonderful times we have spent together with the whole family gathered around the TV. Nobody wants to leave home at night because we would rather watch "The Honeymooners," "Your Show of Shows," "Liberace," and just about everything else. Popcorn and fudge, red apples and popcorn, ice-cream sundaes and root beer floats disappear like magic.

Mom and Dad gave us their picture for Christmas—something we had wanted for a long time.

Kirby and Larry played basketball most of the day and Linda enjoyed her new clock radio. In the evening, Jerry and Jean came to pick up Linda and they went skating. They built a bonfire and Linda got a bad case of poison ivy and had to be taken to the doctor.

Jerry's gifts consisted of things he could take with him in his new way of life. I was unable to sleep when I went to bed. I just wanted to hang on to Christmas, for I dreaded what the new year would bring.

1954

*L*ife has a way of settling into a new pattern after its routine has been disturbed. A heart can be so sad when the first nestling is gone. For a long time I seemed to live in a vacuum where everything was unreal.

Our Jerry is gone. I know other mothers have experienced the same kind of sleeplessness as I, and the drone of a plane or the voice of a locomotive is a mournful sound.

Thousands of mothers before me have suffered the same uncertainties of the future and have also put faith in Almighty God the care for those away from us.

Jerry went to Ft. Leonard Wood, Missouri, and after eight weeks we were allowed to visit him. Jeanie, Kirby and Linda Day went with us. Kirby had missed Jerry so much. Their room was so empty without him. Kirby is a quiet boy and doesn't say much, but the joy on his face at getting to go needed no words.

Two happy boys greeted us when we finally found them. Jerry looked and looked as though he could never get his eyes full. We went to the barracks where we were to stay and two hungry boys dug into the basket from home! Jerry ate fried chicken, sandwiches and hickory nut cake until it almost stuck out of his ears but all Dave Gilbert ate was bread, butter and peanut butter! We weren't allowed off the post so we spent all our time there. It didn't matter because "place" didn't mean a thing. Just seeing our son was what mattered.

On Sunday Jean dressed up in her new taffeta coat that she had made especially to wear for him. It was cold as whiz, but she declared through blue lips and chattering teeth that she was plenty warm in her summer finery while I was freezing in my winter ones!

We said goodbye at midnight and left at 6:00 the next morning. The pretty little girls of the day before were crumpled in a sad heap in the back seat. Their noses were red and their eyes were swollen. We hated to leave them, too, but felt very fortunate that we got to see them at all.

In eight more weeks he was home on furlough. Jim tried on all his gear and said it just fit him, although the coat dragged the floor and if it hadn't been for his nose the hat would have sat down on his shoulders! We had a wonderful two weeks. Jerry bought a ring and we were all happy about the girl he had chosen.

In June, Linda, Jean, Jim, Elmer and I went to Camp Gordon to visit Jerry.

When we moved from town our beautiful green carpet had to be cut to fit our living room and a big piece was left over. After Grandpa was gone we had an empty room at the north end of our small living room that would sure be nice added to our living room! I had been waiting to cover the dark green paint on our walls—well, no use trying to explain why. I had the "urge" again!

Linda and I started moving furniture "out" and "up." Jim didn't say much until we moved the TV set. When he found out it wouldn't be hooked up 'til who knows when, he was very unhappy and tore out to meet his Dad and Kirby when they came from work. "They just tore the whole house to pieces and I can't watch

TV!" This time there was another highly perturbed member of the family and he said, "Now you can just wait 'til I get good and ready to put that back together again!"—so we spent several weeks just waiting and hoping and sitting on the rolled-up carpet, but we had a lot of light in the room after the wall was out.

When life gets dark and you are in the shadows, it is always good to find a speck of light somewhere and concentrate on it! I concentrated about three months on the view out of the north and west windows, disregarding the unpatched plaster, the sunken place in the floor where the hardwood didn't meet, the green paint on the wall at one end and faded flowers on the paper at the other end.

I was glad to escape and go to Camp Gordon. Everything was in order there which is more than I can say about the place I left.

I don't think the Packard likes to travel. We had to lay over on the way to Ft. Leonard Wood to have its insides examined and after a surgical procedure on both the car and our finances, we went on our way.

This time the lights kept going out and that is pretty scary on a rainy night. We stopped earlier than planned and did the remainder of our traveling in the daylight, which meant the "first sight of the whites of their eyes" in the morning to the last readable road sign at night. Elmer hated that car and I don't think it liked him very well either!

Jerry went from Camp Gordon to Ft. Lewis, Washington, where they made an M.P. out of him. We were lucky enough to have him home for Christmas. He arrived on December 8th and was much surprised at the new living room. It was all back together again and was well worth the wait. It was beautiful and it was wonderful not to have to waste that piece of carpet!

Jerry and Jean were married December 18th. Jean was a pretty bride in her beige lace dress. Jerry was married in his uniform. Bill

Murphy from Chicago was his best man. Carol Gilbert was Jean's maid of honor.

Christmas of '54 was wonderful. Now I'm a mother-in-law! Jerry left on the 28th.

1955

As I look back over the past year, a lot has happened—yet, on the surface, life has gone on much the same. Jerry was sent to Korea in February. Duff landed in Germany and ran across and became good friends with Bill Murphy, Jerry's buddy from Chicago. We hope Jerry will be home for Christmas but if he isn't, it won't be too long afterward. We have been busy people this summer. Linda and Kirby are both working. I have been busy in Eastern Star and am thankful for the time has gone so fast. Here it is nearly Christmas time again.

Linda worked at the drug store and Kirby worked for Bill Thomas. He likes the farm. Jim and I held the fort at home.

On March 27th, we had a terrible ice storm. I was to have been installed as Worthy Matron of Eastern Star. It had to be canceled until the 21st. I was escorted by my tall son Kirby, Jim greeted me with a kiss and Jean pinned a lovely corsage on my gown. Elmer sang a song and recited one of my own poems to me! Linda played the piano. It was so beautiful, I shall remember it always!

Jean has been trying unsuccessfully to find a place to live before Jerry comes home. I am confident the Good Lord had a hand in it the way it turned out. One day Jean's mother called me to come to the coil factory where she worked. The grapevine there had circulated the news that Merle and Hazel Brunson were moving. We got on the ball and when Jean came home from work she had a home of her own! If we had dilly-dallied, Bill Randol would have beaten us to it!

It seemed that Christmas would never come and when it did, no Jerry came! Jean wouldn't open her presents and we rewrapped most of ours and put them back under the tree to wait for Jerry. Kirby and Jim got a box of tricks and had lots of fun with it, especially the bottle of ink seemingly spilled on Linda's new sweater!

This has been a nice summer for Kirby. He bought "Strawberry" and enjoys riding and caring for her. Jim Woodward keeps his horse here too and they have great times. They are contented to wade mud and whatever at horse shows.

Linda was a busy girl in school. She was a yell leader and Mr. France's office girl. School is too confining for Kirby. He'd rather spend time with his horse!

Jim is doing better since he got his "spelling" pills. Our doctor said he needed a round of worm medicine. He gave him two sacks of pills and Jim ran out of the waiting room and embarrassed Linda and Kirby half to death by announcing in a loud voice, "See, I got two sacks of pills! I've got WORMS!" I had to send the pills to school with him and told him to tell the kids they were "spelling" pills because they would help him spell better!

Kirby and his pals Larry, Jim W., Max and Earl spend a lot of time upstairs painting and constructing planes and ships. It's more like a garbage dump from all the debris I sweep out! They eat everything that isn't nailed down. I guess I wouldn't have it any other way. I know where they are.

We spent Christmas with Mom and Dad but came home fairly early and went to bed. Jean stayed all night and with Linda and

Kirby painted model planes until almost morning. Poor little Jim! He is the only one left to hit the floor before daybreak. The others are too grown up and know that it will keep until they get enough sleep. I wanted to chase him back to bed but his daddy said, "No, let's just get up. That wouldn't be fair because we got up for all the others!"—so, a bedraggled crew circled the Christmas tree in the wee hours and explored the packages. Daddy got a big office desk and Jim had more fun with the box than he did with his toys!

We had gone to bed on New Year's Eve but I heard the girls come home and join Jim, Kirby and Jim Woodward in the kitchen eating soup. Linda yelled, "*Mom!*" and the chairs scraped on the floor. It was such a happy commotion I knew immediately what it was! I ran to the stairway and there at the bottom stood our Jerry! Home at last! Such a burden was lifted from my heart, I bawled like I never did all the time he was gone!

With thankful hearts we were soon all gathered around the Christmas tree again. Not much sleep the rest of the night. Jean had to show him the little house he didn't know he had and was he ever proud! What a happy, happy time! Helping them was like getting married all over again.

Elmer and I celebrated our 25th wedding anniversary with a Coke at Louie Lines' filling station. Some time earlier he had given me a beautiful ring with five diamonds in it. I am very proud of him and his thoughtfulness!

1956

*W*e have a sadness in our lives. Our friend of many years, Agnes Grover, died from cancer on December 12th. She and Paul have been good friends for a long time. We will never forget our fishing trips we had with them. Agnes suffered so much that it was a relief to see her at rest. Herbert is married and has three children but she will never have the joy of watching them grow up. Paul and Carol won't have a very happy Christmas this year. Agnes was a hard worker and wonderful housekeeper. She and Paul both loved kids but were given only one. They adopted Carol when she was a baby and brought a lot of joy to their lives.

We are so thankful for our blessings of good health for us and our children. All goes well with the newlyweds and they bought the little home they started out in February.

Linda Gay graduated in May and had a nice trip through the eastern states. She secured a good job at General Electric soon as she graduated and is making good money. Kirby is happy working for his dad this summer. He, Jerry and Roger Kinsey work together. Kirby was sixteen in September. He sold his horse and bought a

Ford. He likes a little girl named Shirley, and can think of more reasons why he must go to Zanesville.

Linda and Don Carl have been dating. She almost missed the boat. Don's friend called Linda and asked if she had any plans for Saturday night. She didn't like him very well, so she said, "I have to babysit with Jim." He said, "Well, Don Carl asked me to call you. He wanted a date!" Linda hung up and was about ready to cry. She had been hoping he would ask her. She said, "Mom, what am I going to do?" I said, "Well, you're going to babysit. If you hadn't lied you would be having a date with Don Carl Saturday night!" The next time she found out who wanted the date and he did ask her again. When he came to pick her up Jim said, "Now, that's what I call a boyfriend!" He is a very nice boy and I have thought so for a long time. He has great ambitions of becoming an engineer and we hope he can someday see his dream come true.

Linda has enjoyed her Christmas shopping with her own money, and brings home some interesting-looking packages that disappear quickly.

I thoroughly enjoy the shopping and planning surprises for those so dear to me, but hope I never forget the reason Christmas came to be. I try to keep Christmas all year in the associations with friends and relatives. The gift of the first Christmas was from the love of God to man. Our gifts to each other should be prompted by the same unselfishness.

This year we enjoyed a bounteous harvest and our cellar and freezer overflow with good things from our garden. It's a good feeling to know I have contributed toward the welfare of my family.

Wilma Johnson and I picked soup beans and I have a good store of them. Josephine and I picked up popcorn in her Uncle's field. I have about fifteen gallons of shelled popcorn! Josephine and I went hickory nut hunting and I have a lot for cookies and fudge.

These are the very best years of my life! Our house is always

"Open House" where our friends or the kids' friends are welcome any time. It is good to sit over a cup of coffee and visit even if there are clothes to be ironed or furniture to be dusted. Good conversations with friends have a way of making the work go twice as fast!

This Christmas was a lovely one. The little live tree stood in front of the big south window. We spent Christmas Eve with Dad and Mom. They were married fifty years in November. Marjorie and I planned a nice party for them at the Dutch Mill. We were all there except Mary and her family. Mom and Dad enjoyed it very much, and I was so happy to do it for them. They have had a hard life and deserve much more than I can ever give them.

We got home early on Christmas Eve. We gathered around the piano and enjoyed our own singing.

Jean asked if we cared if they came out and stayed all night. Of course we were so happy they wanted to come. We arose early and opened our gifts then had breakfast and lots of fun afterward. Linda went with Don to his home for dinner. Kirby went to Shirley's house. He asked his dad what he thought of his girl and Elmer pleased him when he said, "If I were sixteen I'd give you competition, my boy!" It is so much fun seeing them grow up. Our little Jim was just ten, and wouldn't trade his TV or his blanket for any girls alive!

This summer the yard mowing has been mostly Jim's job. I help out when he needs me. One day this summer he was mowing and I was high up in the cherry tree picking cherries, when a boy Jim's age stopped and helped him finish mowing the yard. When I got out of the tree at noon to fix lunch they were busy playing with cars and trucks by the kitchen window. I invited him to stay for lunch and he accepted. He was quite a talkative little fellow and informed us he had ridden to Huntington that morning and traded in his old bike and rode his new one past our place on his way home. (We live eight miles from Huntington.)

We had new peas for lunch and Jim said he didn't want any. Our visitor said, "Now, Jim, eat your peas. They are good for you and you ought to be thankful you've got peas to eat!" We talked of many things and after lunch was over and we had admired his new bike he said he believed he'd just go swimming since he was so close to the pool and away he went! I asked Jim who he was and Jim said, "Heck, I dunno, I think he goes to our school!"

Later on in the day from my roost in the top of the cherry tree, I heard someone singing at the top of his voice. When he came into view and saw me he waved and waved his little arm and called to me in a loud voice, "So long—so long and thanks for lunch!" He rode out of my life on his new bicycle and I never saw him again and never knew his name. Wherever he is I hope he never loses his zest for living and his carefree, jaunty spirit.

1957

I hardly know where to start. This has been such a full and busy year! Here I am on Saturday evening, December 28th, trying to remember all the important events of the year. The first part was very unhappy and trying but I know now that "However bitter may be the cup which our Heavenly Father gives us, it will, in the end, overflow with blessings, rich, abounding and eternal."

The thing that happened was that we have a son-in-law. That "Now, that's what I call a boy friend" turned into a husband. They also were married in the Methodist Church. It was a lovely, simple wedding and I was proud of the beautiful bride who walked down the aisle, but I was also proud of her daddy who walked beside her. What a good companion he has been! How many lovely experiences we have shared! How handsome he looked to me escorting our only daughter on her wedding day!

The days were so busy I hardly had time to miss her, but when 5:00 came a feeling of loneliness settled on my heart when she didn't come home from work. She is very happy. She has been home often this summer and has canned a lot of good things for winter.

Jeanie would have loved to spend some time with us canning and nut hunting but she is a busy girl all day. Don and Linda live in New Haven and Jim spent a few days there when we went on our nice trip with Ray and Fern. Work has been plentiful and Jerry is beginning to be good help. Elmer can get away a few days now and then.

Kirby is now the proud owner of a blue Studebaker. His romance has its ups and downs, but life is great for all of us.

Linda gave us a little grandson in November. He was the nicest package we had for Christmas. Mitchell Delayne didn't care much about Santa Claus. We love him so much. Don loves his little son and his mother does too. I know he is a lucky little boy!

We have much to be thankful for this Christmas. Mom and Dad moved to Markle on Thanksgiving Day and are so proud of their little home with the first bathroom they ever had! Dad said, "Here I am seventy-five years old and last night was the first time I was ever in a real bathtub!" Mom said he sat in there for over an hour! We are waiting for news of the birth of Mary's baby. We are also happy to know we will be grandparents again next year. Jerry and Jean are so happy! Their baby is already dear to me although it can be no bigger than a marshmallow! Next year Mitchie will have a little first cousin. (That confuses Jim. He thinks Cathy is his first cousin and Paul his second cousin and Dennis his third cousin!)

My thoughts turn to Kirby and I wish for him the same happiness Jerry and Linda have found. Jean and Don, I consider as my children too and I know that when and who Kirby chooses will be just as dear. He sings baritone in the school quartet and they meet here sometimes and beat out a tune on the old piano. Elmer and I both enjoy these times. Jim is a TV fan and anything that moves on the screen is his "favorite program!" He will be a Boy Scout soon. He will be our third Boy Scout and we have one Girl Scout. Ernie Laymon put in many hours as the Boy Scout leader and he is a good one.

116

The kids were all home all night Christmas. I treasure this happiness for I know it won't happen too many times.

We enjoyed our breakfast of fruit cup, ham, eggs, homemade biscuits and Christmas cookies. Everyone had dates elsewhere for the day, but Elmer, Jim and I had a good time by ourselves.

We slept all afternoon! In the evening Linda and Maxine (Don's sister) came and we had a nice visit. Jean and Jerry ate supper with us and we put together Jim's big jigsaw puzzle.

It has been a lovely day. The coming week will be spent reminiscing and looking at all the cards again. Then it will all disappear and a clean swept house will bring us back to ordinary living. It still seems strange to sit at the table with only four of us, but we are lucky. We get to see the married kids often.

1958

Christmas this year finds another angel on our family tree. Little Alfreda Janelle was born on August 14th. Her big blue eyes took in everything and I couldn't help wondering what she was thinking. She sat in her basket and watched "first cousin" scrambling around in all the paper and ribbons. I know next year she will participate.

We were up at 5:00 as usual on this beautiful morning. Maybe in four more years we will get to sleep. Jim will be sixteen then and will probably have other interests than what is under the tree. We hated to open the packages. They looked so pretty! Jean and I had lots of fun wrapping Linda's bedspread. We wrapped it around a two-by-four and dressed it up like a girl. Nobody could guess what secrets the tall blonde was hiding. Don worked for a long time wrapping Linda's sewing machine. We had some strange packages under our tree and lots of fun opening them.

Don and Linda moved their trailer here in January so they are close to us. I am determined that Don will never have any mother-in-law trouble! I shall try to keep my lip zipped and my nose where it belongs! That is a very strenuous resolution for someone as knowledgeable as I with all my worldly experience!

Don is studying hard to attain his goal in life and I feel that such determination will be rewarded.

Jerry, Jean and Janelle stayed all night. Kirby crawled out of bed early and brought Shirley home before we opened gifts. She was really surprised when she got a cedar chest.

We are so fortunate to have been blessed with a family. There have been lean times but when we see their happy faces around the Christmas tree we realize that the only thing we lack an abundance of is money. Somehow you don't miss it so much when you have all the things it can't buy! Looking at our two dear grandbabies helps me understand why Elmer's mother was so anxious for a grandchild and I'm glad I didn't disappoint her!

This summer my dreams of a new house started coming true. My husband is a carpenter, and I've heard it noised around that he is pretty good. I am within three or four months of finding out!

For six years we have been discussing this old house and what we were going to do with it in the way of remodeling. As usual it seemed like such a task that we kept putting it off, until the freezer made the decision for us. It started to get cantankerous around Christmas. About a week later it just simply died! It is a sorrowful sight seeing plump strawberries thaw and wilt in their own juice and smell the fish sending out signals that if something isn't done immediately somebody is going to be sorry! An S.O.S. to Clair Geiger soon brought a new freezer to our door and it was a thing of beauty! In the plans for our new kitchen it was to sit beside our refrigerator. That appliance bears the scars of seventeen years of child raising and sure did look down in the mouth beside that new freezer so we bought a new one. They were both so beautiful that they deserved better surroundings than this ugly old kitchen! I informed my husband that he would just have to help me wash down the high ceilings and walls before I could apply a new coat of paint. You'd never dream to look at him to what lengths he would go to get out of helping wash that ceiling! Without any forewarning whatsoever he commanded, "Make up your mind how you want this kitchen fixed!" I was catapulted headfirst into a world of drawing boards, scale rules, templates, clippings I've saved for twenty years, a dozen catalogues of modern kitchens, some dating back to 1936, blueprints of kitchens he had built for other women and the deep down fear that if I failed to come up with a plan soon, he would change his mind! I felt like I was dreaming and that any minute I would fall from my rosy cloud and land with a thud in my old high-ceilinged, thin-plastered, windswept kitchen.

I say "windswept" because on a day when the wind comes from the west the linoleum raises two or three inches off the floor and I can actually see out of the high windows!

However, time proved this was no dream and when the new windows were installed I looked out on a new scene. The kitchen was still dark so we installed another window the next week. Now I can wave to my neighbor! After another week the door was moved. (Don't get the wrong idea. It doesn't take him a week to put in a window or a door, but a carpenter's wife gets her work done by one nail at a time! After working at the job site all day he did what he could evenings and weekends. He worked hard—we both worked hard. There were many things I could do and I did them!) My hindsight told me that a jalousie door would leave in more light, but he said the frame was wrong for it. That was the day before Easter. My husband is a very thoughtful man but he can never think to buy a gift or a card for an "occasion." After watching me fix Easter baskets for all the kids, including him, he said, "Honey, I didn't get you anything for Easter!" I soothed his feelings as best I could. Then he put his arm around me and said, "You can have the jalousie door if you want it. It won't take too much work to change the frame!" I thought to myself, "My dear, your ears are getting longer!" and forever afterward when I look at that new door

I will remember how I saw it first as a promise under the arm of my Easter bunny!

Today, a week later, the new kitchen is very real. The drop ceilings are in and wiring done. From my perch on the kitchen stool I survey my surroundings and begin to wonder, "How long, how long?"

We never move when we remodel—we just redistribute. All the things I knew I wouldn't need, all the things I thought I wouldn't, and all the things I knew I would need later but would come up for at the time were hauled up to Linda's empty room. Now half the things I knew I wouldn't need have been brought down and half the things I left down have been carted back upstairs! All the appliances have been moved into the 12' x 14' utility room. Going clockwise around the room I'll draw a verbal picture of it. On the newspaper-covered drier I find the electric skillet, a sack of garden seeds, a can of Lux, a recipe file upon which is a Boy Scout handbook, a bottle of hand lotion, a half-empty sack of cashews, and a brand new fluorescent light bulb! Above it hangs this year's calendar, some wire racks from the old freezer, and a black plywood tray that Kirby's little inexperienced hands made eleven years ago. It is decorated with golden hearts and the words, "Dear Father and Mother."

Next to the dryer is a utility cabinet, on top of which is the electric deep fryer, on top of which are three empty egg cartons. Squeezed between this and the new refrigerator are two chairs. The new appliances share the burden in this mess. On top of one is a sack of beans, a box of napkins, half a box of crackers, a box of Aydes and empty freezer boxes. The other holds freezer wrap, spice racks from the old cupboard, light bulbs, wonder rice and a box of cereal. Beside the freezer is the ironer where the bread box rests, on top of which is a dispenser for three kinds of paper, the sugar and flour containers. Behind all this on the radiator are stored all the gadgets for the new cupboards. In front of the ironer stands the cartoned front panel for the dishwasher. Turning east I find the old fridge on top of which rests the mixer and inside of which are all the dishes we need at present. Next is a carton holding the new stove and another the new sink. Next is the old gas stove, which has seen us through so many sleet storms. It holds a teakettle, a can of "Fluffo"—though nothing golden is about to happen in this place!—the salt and pepper, a clean jelly glass and a dirty milk bottle. Its insides are crammed with the necessary pans to see us through in the cooking department. Behind the stove is the washer sprouting evidence that another washday is upon us! Beside it are two twin tubs over which is a board that serves as a temporary (I hope) worktable, which holds the blessed electric percolator and a stray pot lid. On the floor is an economy-size soapbox, the bleach bottle, the mop bucket, two wastepaper baskets and some leftover metal from the installation of the ventilating fan. In the window above are four fruit jars holding four sprouting sweet potatoes which we will plant this year to raise more sweet potatoes—four of which will end up in the same window next year to start the cycle all over again. In the corner are two shelves. One holds a drinking glass, laundry starch, coffee can, scouring powders, a spoon and a rock which our young rock collector brought home. The top shelf carries a cargo of Spic & Span, laundry rinse, dog food, the iron, and the toaster with its tail wrapped around its middle. This completes the scene except for two yardsticks stuck behind a water pipe and a wilted apron dangling from a nail.

In the center of the room (if you can believe there is one) stands the little, white enamel-topped table which graced our first kitchen twenty-eight years ago. When the four of us sit there to eat we just put our feet in each other's laps and dig in, getting it over with as soon as possible! Just try *cooking* a meal in this place if you think the eating is tough! There is room for one to work and that one should be just half my size. Have you ever been in a hurry to get a meal because one son has a date, the other one wants to eat before his favorite TV program comes on and your husband has to go to Lodge and everything seems well in hand 'til you discover you can't find the cinnamon? Have you ever looked on everything, under everything, and crawled around on your hands and knees thinking it may have fallen off of something and have a thought strike you and you trudge shame-faced upstairs to where you remember having put it? Have you ever stooped over to remove the meat from the broiler, crash the silence when your protruding behind came in contact with the just-set supper table and sent the forks and knives flying in all directions? Have you ever estimated the damage while you rub your sore spot to find the sugar has spilled into the butter and the jelly, which was wobbly anyway, has leaned over and laid in the peas? If you have experienced any small part of this, you will understand my determination to move out the next time we remodel if I have to set up my headquarters under a tree!

This Christmas of 1958 finds us in our new kitchen and do I ever love the new dishwasher! Elmer gave me a corner cupboard for the dining room. I hope before the next phase of this undertaking arrives my scratches and bruises have healed and my charley horses have straightened themselves out and that I have some fingernails!

1959

This was a summer with many changes in our lives. Don and Linda moved to Lafayette in September. They will be there 'til Don finishes his schooling at Purdue. I miss my little Mitchie. They hadn't been there very long 'til the little soul fell and a sliver of glass penetrated his eye. We were all so upset we didn't know what to do, and hurried down to see him. He didn't know us but when he saw my old brown purse he pointed and said, "do-do." He always knew Grandma carried a treat for him and he knew us then. My heart ached so for the little fellow I would gladly have given him one of my eyes. Jim wanted to give one of his, he felt so terrible. (If it had happened years later I know they could have saved it but laser beam hadn't been discovered yet or hadn't been perfected.)

Our sadness was alleviated somewhat. Our baby Jeff was born October 16th. Now little Janelle has a playmate. He couldn't get used to his new home and cried the first night. Janelle tried to see what was going on and fell out of bed on her head! Jerry was trying to sleep but two crying babies brought him out to see what was going on! Not much sleep for any of us the rest of the night! Little Nell stayed with Grandma while Mom was in the hospital. We feel so lucky they are so near that we can watch them grow. Jerry fenced in their back yard and the babies will have a nice place to play.

Kirby and Elmer worked over by Hartford City remodeling a house this summer. Kirby has had unhappiness because the girl he wants doesn't seem to want him. The people they worked for had a lot of horses and a girl his age. He worked up the courage to ask her for a date, and was to go to her house on Saturday night. I was pressing his suit and talking to him about her when he informed me he wasn't going! "Not going!" I said. "Mom, if I can't have Shirley I don't want anybody!" So, I guess he was more interested in the horses than the girl. He had started to her house and stopped at Adelphia Gardens and called Shirley. Their difficulties were solved, so he called the horse rider and told her he wouldn't be down Saturday night. I don't suppose she cared because I think she liked horses better than boys! I thought to myself "three down one to go!" We are so happy with all three choices. We will have our Jim for a long time yet. He is thirteen and is contented to play with his dog and watch TV.

We had so many things to be thankful for as we gathered around our tree this year. Three darling babies and a dear girl who would someday belong to our family!

The one surprise package under the tree was for Don and Linda. We knew they were having a rough time so we bought beef and put it in the locker for them. We wrapped the tail up with a note saying the rest of it was in the locker downtown! It was such a joy having them all home once again. I know that someday they can't spend Christmas with us so I hug these moments close to my heart and am truly thankful for these precious times!

1960

Kirby and Shirley were married in a beautiful ceremony in the Zanesville church. I helped Helen decorate for the reception and it was the last appearance of my antique compote. I had hoped to use it at all the kids' weddings, but alas! It was not to be! During the summer I was making a flower arrangement and the dish slipped and broke into a pile of splinters. Now Jim won't have it at his wedding. The church was beautiful, but no more so than the two who spoke their vows to each other. I can sit dry-eyed through a funeral but a wedding just forces the tears out of me so fast I can't catch them and they run down on my finery.

There just always has to be something funny happen to relieve the tension of the day. I was giving Ed and Elmer the once-over before we were ushered in and Ed had his cummerbund down low under his stomach and Elmer had his studs in upside down!

At Don and Linda's wedding Kirby called about twenty minutes before the ceremony was to begin and said the flowers weren't in there yet! I nearly lost my "cool" and tried to reach the florist. Kirby called back and said they had just arrived.

As Linda walked down the aisle Jerry whispered to me and said, "What's wrong with her? Look at her back!" It was red as fire! That's one frustration I could have missed because I was still so shaken up about the flowers that I hadn't noticed!

The boys had laughed about an article we read in the paper about a groom kneeling at the altar and some prankster having written "Help" on the bottom of his shoe. I had an eerie feeling it was about to happen again, but it didn't.

The morning of Jerry and Jean's wedding the roads were a glare of ice. Their reception was at the Union Town Club House. Elmer went with me and we slid to Fort Wayne to pick up the punch, bowls and dishes. We prayed all the way home we'd stay in the road.

We collected all the necessities and went to decorate. Bless Mary, Floyd and Dean Thomas. They came down and helped us.

Jerry's friend Bill Murphy and his girlfriend Juli came to the wedding so we had to hurry home to fix lunch. Our house was full, our hearts were full and our hands were full! The reception was lovely and we all enjoyed it. After the bride and groom left we loaded up all the presents, the decorations, the waste paper and dirty dishes, and headed for home. We spent what was left of the rest of the night washing dishes and repacking them. We fell into bed at midnight exhausted but happy!

Kirby and Shirley opened presents for a long time but finally got started on their trip south. They visited Mary and Raymond, but they were anxious to get home to their apartment and didn't stay away long. A sweet little house in town became available and they moved before they had hardly gotten settled. The little house was ideal for a young couple.

This has certainly been a busy year. Jim and I worked at Tom Bomar's grocery store, and between trying to find time to play with Jeff and Janelle, making trips to Lafayette and enjoying Kirby and Shirley, the time just flew past! Our garden missed us and became overgrown and crowded with weeds, but Jim managed to keep the lawn mowed.

Mitchell's doctor advised Don and Linda to take him to Chicago to see a specialist. Don was in a critical test period in college, so he was unable to go. Elmer was covered up with work and couldn't go, so after many serious instructions and directions and maps from Lawrence Warner and Howard Anderson, Jim and I took off for Lafayette. With a much-pregnant Linda and little Mitchell we were on our way to Chicago! Never having driven in a city larger than Fort Wayne, I was scared to death!

We made the trip just fine but about twenty minutes after we got parked the officials shut off Michigan Avenue for a parade! Lawrence and Howard had failed to explain what to do in case this had happened before we got there! I had asked God for help and guidance in my prayers the night before, and He was certainly on hand as He always is! Everybody was glad to see us safely home and I'll confess I was mighty glad to be there too.

This year five blessed babies stayed all night and added joy around the Christmas tree! Courtney and Byron were born fifteen days apart. They were too little to know what was going on but the other three were aware. Jeff and Janelle wore their sweet little pink and blue snowsuits. Jeff is a shy little fellow and hangs pretty close to his mom. Mitchell and Janelle played in the paper and boxes after the gifts were opened. Breakfast was pretty hectic being prepared with these little cousins chasing each other around the kitchen but we managed to find a place to eat around the card tables. What a wonderful time! How dear they all are! How much we have to look forward to with two little boys sleeping in their baskets, one little boy a year old, my precious namesake almost two years old and "first cousin" just past three. Best of all we still have Jim who is just fourteen. My dear husband is a busy man and works too hard. We are getting ahead a little—just fast enough to hope that before long we can remodel our house to match our pretty kitchen. I have enjoyed it so much, especially the dishwasher. I was so thankful for the new kitchen that I decided I would do without the dishwasher, but Elmer insisted and am I ever glad! Now on canning day I can put all the jars in and do them all at once. They are clean and ready to receive our good food we store for the winter.

This Christmas of 1960 was a wonderful day. They were all with us Christmas Eve and all night. Christmas Day, they all go to the other parents' homes and we just rest and relive all the happenings of the day and night!

On June 30th this spring our town was nearly destroyed by fire. It started in the old sale barn back of the buildings on the south side of the street and would have destroyed the whole town if it hadn't been for Ralph Reed and his ham radio. The phone lines were burned at the beginning of the fire and there was no way to call for help. Ralph rushed to his home and sent the message, "This is an emergency. We need help! Half the town of Markle is on fire!" With that his radio went dead but his message was picked up by Wendell Larimore just east of town who relayed the message. Help came from Huntington, Uniondale, Bluffton, Ossian and Warren. It was a terrible sight! We were eating supper when we heard the sirens. I had Mitchie that week, and we were like everybody else, we jumped in the car and went to see what was going on—and there was plenty going on! Traffic was backed up in all four directions and had to be rerouted. When Jim came home that night he said, "I know what I'm going to be when I grow up! I'm going to be a traffic cop—I just held up my hand and those *big* trucks stopped right now!"

The old sale barn will be missed for it holds a lot of good memories for a lot of people. At one time it was a skating rink where the town kids and a lot of grownups, too, had a lot of fun.

My special memories are of the year 1928 when Elmer and I had just started dating. He, his dad and his uncle Pat remodeled this same building. It was just across the alley from the back door of the restaurant where I was working. Sometimes Elmer absented himself from the job and appeared through the back door to help me wash dishes! One day Uncle Pat came over to buy his chewing tobacco and with that impish grin I came to know so well, announced for the whole establishment to hear that they were having an awful time keeping Elmer on the job and that he just bet there was a girl that he was slipping over here to see and wondered if I might know who it could be! Of course my face turned as red as my hair, and I was teased until they got some other poor soul to pick on!

I never tired of listening to, or about, Pat! He was always a happy-go-lucky guy and I think he must have coined the phrase, "Always leave them laughing!"

1961

This has been quite a summer. Jim got in on the tearing out of walls this time. We enlarged the back porch and made it into a utility room, and built a garage. Then it was time to "redistribute" again. Jim and I worked our tails off moving most of the furniture. The south end of the utility room was his bedroom, the south end of the garage was the living room and the north end was our bedroom. (No doors anywhere except to the outside!) We moved the concrete laundry tubs to the garage and it served as a bathtub all summer. The only privacy we had was to wait 'til everybody was gone, then step upon a chair, climb into one compartment of the tub and sit on a stool placed in the other compartment. Then with the dry towel hanging over the edge, you proceeded to wash one square foot of skin at a time and this was possible only by being somewhat of a contortionist. Usually after reaching for the soap for the second square foot it shot out of your wet hands and landed on the garage floor ten feet away! One time after Jerry, Kirby and Gary Carl had finished work for the day, Jim and Elmer went to the lumberyard. I thought it was a good chance for a leisurely bath and just got started when Gary yelled,

"Alfreda!" I didn't dare not answer for fear he would come looking for me. As I grabbed for the towel it slid to the floor far beyond my reach! I was horrified but had to answer. Gary had left some of his tools in Elmer's truck. I yelled out, "Hurry down to the lumber yard, you can catch him there—*hurry!*" I don't remember whether I bathed again that summer or not!

Once when we lived in Buckeye I rigged up a shower on the back porch. It was a bucket (set up on a shelf) with a hose attached. I had bathed Jerry and said, "Now, you run out and play while Mama takes her bath." I was enjoying my shower when a little knock sounded on the screen door. I called out "Just a minute, honey, I'll soon be through!" Instead of my little boy answering, Ralph Poulson yelled through the screen, "Where's Elmer?" It's enough to make one give up bathing forever!

In June Don graduated from Purdue and three days afterward moved to Brownsburg to a trailer court. Don had secured a job in Indianapolis.

The remodeling was slow and awfully hard work for Jim and me. It was our job to load the trash and move it out into the field to be burned. He loved it because he got to drive the truck! I must say he earned the privilege.

We had sealed the doorway between the kitchen and old dining room and got along very well. We had a clean place to cook, eat and a place to wash and dry our dirty clothes in the beautiful new automatic washer and dryer. We had a decent place to sleep, so what more could anyone want? Well, maybe one thing—a bathtub!

I thought I would surely die of happiness when the fireplace was done. It was so beautiful and I had waited so long! The set of fireplace fixtures Elmer gave me for Christmas 1947 had long rusted away and had never been used. They did, however, keep my dream alive!

I had a pile of kindling ready when Dale Neusbaum laid the last brick, but he informed me I had to wait 'til it was thoroughly dried—about three weeks! It was such a busy summer going here and there choosing drapes, colors, carpeting and all the other things. I looked and looked for drapery material, then the minute I laid eyes on it I knew it was for me! I have never seen anything before or since so beautiful as they were. A terrible week followed the purchase of them. I had saved $150 to buy them and it slipped out the side of a pocket in my purse! I didn't know the purse was split 'til I got home and discovered my loss. I was depressed. I called every place I could think of having been without success. Then on Friday night (a week later) I dreamed the *News-Banner* had called and said they had some money for me. On Saturday, Don and Linda came, I told her about it. She said, "Why don't' you call them?" I hadn't put any stock in dreams but called them anyway. I could not believe my ears when they told me they had been waiting for a week for somebody to claim money found on the streets of Bluffton! I described the papers it was wrapped in and came home with my drapery money! I am now a believer of miracles and the owner of a new purse!

This Christmas of 1961 finds us with our beloved family gathered around the Christmas tree in front of the new fireplace! The little cousins again played in the paper and two little cousins watched from perches in their high chairs.

Jim rooted everybody out early and the young parents all were ready to break his neck and threatened him with, "Just you wait! We will get even with you sometime!"

After breakfast all the little ones were bundled up and taken to the other grandpas' and grandmas' houses for them to enjoy. Don and Linda stayed all night again, which made our Christmas last a day longer.

I always have to loosen my fingers one by one to make them let go of Christmas!

1962

*J*im was sixteen years old on December 7th. Why start out with this statement? Because we nearly lost him on Mother's Day! It started out as a beautiful day. It was so warm and the flowers were so beautiful. Jerry and Jean had gone to a picnic at the park with her family. Kirby had a job on the railroad and had gone out on a run. They had just bought their first home. Don and Linda came in the afternoon. Jim gave me a pot of white mums for Mother's Day and kissed me goodbye before he went to help his friend at the filling station downtown. Linda, Shirley and I had gone down to see Shirley and Kirb's new home. I was sitting in the porch swing with Mitchie beside me. Elmer drove up and had the grayest, awfulest look on his face! He told me, "Jim has been shot!" I was paralyzed with shock and fear as we raced toward Bluffton. The Mother's Day kiss was all I could remember and kept asking myself "was it his last good-bye?" I next saw him lying on the operating table wrapped in a plastic sheet with his life's blood dripping down in a bucket on the floor! Dr. Max Gitlin came out and said "My God, Elmer, is that your boy?" We knew there was little hope for him! "His only chance is to get him to Lutheran Hospital in Fort Wayne," Dr. Gitlin told us, and he was soon back in the ambulance with Dr. Gitlin and me beside him. Before we got to Ossian, the ambulance blew a tire and we went from side to side in the road. I remember crying aloud, "*Oh, God, save us!*" Jim opened his eyes and said, "It's all right Mom." Afterward he said that was the last he remembered. We tore through Ossian, Waynedale and Fort Wayne with a police escort after being transferred to an ambulance from Ossian! When they wheeled him to emergency I knew I'd never see him alive again and was too numb to pray. It was a long, long wait. As the hours stretched on, our family was all there to give us support. Jerry drove Dr. Gitlin's car and followed the ambulance. I don't remember who was with him besides Elmer and Jean, but they all got there some way! Shirley called Kirby and he was on the next train leaving Lima. Ed and Helen took care of the babies. Don and Linda were in shorts, which at that time were not worn at hospitals! After a long, long time Dr. McCechron informed us Jim had lived through and all we had to worry about was infection. He had had a very narrow escape. The shot was from a British rifle and had gone in at his shoulder between a vital nerve and artery—a place impossible to get between—but it did! It hit his shoulder blade, glanced off and went through his lung. I don't know how but it came out his back within a hair's breadth of the spine and left a hole the doctor said was big enough that he could have put his fist in! Then he added, "This boy has had good care. His strength and vitality is all that has saved him. You must feed him very well!" We did feed him very well—good wholesome milk, eggs, fruits and vegetables. When I see puny little kids who won't eat vegetables, meat and all the foods to make strong bodies, I shake in my shoes! What will happen to them if disaster strikes and their bodies have to withstand the shock and long recovery that Jim's body did?

Jim was in intensive care for eight days. I felt like a robot there in the hospital. They told us to go home and we went. When the shock was over I called myself all kinds of a fool for not staying all night. They said, "We will call you!" I spent a sleepless night and would have felt much better on a hard chair in the waiting room. Don and Linda stayed all night. Nobody was able to sleep.

Jim did recover without any ill affects. Dr. Gitlin could not believe it. For as long as he lived, whenever he saw either of us he asked, "How is Jim?" and still shook his head in disbelief.

Jim was awarded his Eagle Scout badge in the autumn and it was presented by Stanley Tobias. Stanley was a Markle boy and once when we lived in town he came to help Jerry and me work in the rock garden. We asked him to stay for dinner. We had fried chicken and all the good things that go with it. Stanley ate so much chicken I jokingly told him, "Stanley, you are going to grow up to be a preacher"—and he did!

Doctor Woods died this summer. It was a tragic loss to our community.

As we gathered around the Christmas tree this year with our whole family there were no words to express the deep thanksgiving in our hearts. We had come through a terrible experience, and here we all were—all fourteen of us. I felt that the Christmas tree was an altar and I gave thanks many times during the season.

1963

This year has been full of excitement. Jim is seventeen and getting awfully anxious for a car.

Don and Linda sold their trailer and moved to Indianapolis. They have a big yard with a nice garden space and a lot of fruit trees and shrubbery. The two little boys have a nice place to play.

When Markle put in a new bridge over the Wabash and rerouted the river, several houses had to be moved or torn down. Vaughn Crown came to our house to talk to Elmer about it, as Hilda's father's house was one of the ones that had to go. They didn't want to tear it down because it was a good solid house made from lumber the likes of which is seldom, if ever, seen these days. He didn't suppose they could ever sell it because the cost of moving it would be prohibitive. About that time Jerry drove in and Elmer had an inspiration. He and Jerry and Vaughn talked for a while and when Jerry left, he had a lot to think about! They owned their little home in town but were outgrowing it and it was also too close to the road for the safety of the little ones. We were anxious for their decision and when it came we were happy. Paul

Brickley sold them two acres and it wasn't long 'til the dirt was flying and a new basement was taking shape. When the tall, old house was set on the foundation, it looked like something out of *Wuthering Heights*, looming tall and stark in a treeless setting without even a bush to tie it to the landscape! It was hard to picture the possibilities, but there were a lot of them. In time they were able to build a two-car garage and a kitchen wing, which was instrumental in bringing it closer to the earth. Today lovely trees and flowers have inured it to its setting and a passerby would think it was built on the site from scratch. Now little Jeff and Janelle have a nice, safe place to play.

Our shop burned July 4th. Hubert Girvin stopped and told us. He called the fire department because I was so shocked I couldn't move! Elmer and I had been home all day but Jim had gone to a 4th celebration unaware that we were having one of our own! Everything was destroyed and Elmer was very depressed. Not only about our loss, but also the loss of faith in an insurance company which had carried the policy for years—even through the time Raymond Stahl had owned it! We could have raised the roof but Bill Hamilton advised us not to. He said the only ones that would make anything out of it would be the lawyers—and he was our lawyer. The adjuster came and I guess he felt sorry for us. He allowed us $2,000, which was only a drop in the bucket toward the rebuilding, but it was better than nothing!

Mom was operated on for gallbladder on November 1st. I stayed with her two days and nights and was rewarded on November 3rd with the news that we had another granddaughter. Sweet little Juli Louise was born. Now Byron has a playmate! After she came home from the hospital, Jim brought his new girlfriend, Sandra Hahn, to meet his new niece and her parents. A flustered Sandy nearly sat on the baby—an embarrassment she never forgot!

I surprised my husband with a birthday party at the Dutch Mill in Bluffton. Afterward we went to Jerry and Jean's and spent the evening having fun. All were there except Don and Linda—it was too far to come over the "Whee" hills (Mitchell always said "Whee" when the car went over a hill, thus the name "Whee Hills").

Mitchell and Janelle are in kindergarten.

One day Jean needed to go to Fort Wayne and I went along. The kids and I sat in the car while she went about her business. Janelle saw a lady coming down the street taking up half the sidewalk. She didn't have much to recommend her in the way of looks. She wore a dingy, old black coat with a ratty, moth-eaten fur collar. Janelle said, "Look, Grandma, that's just buiful—just buiful!" It must be true that "beauty is in the eye of the beholder." For Christmas Grandma made her dolly a "buiful" black coat with a fur collar.

Little Juli was the baby angel this year. What joy a new baby brings! Not one little redhead has made an appearance yet! I have been so proud of our redheaded four that I would welcome a few more. Of course they are all very dear, no matter the color of their hair!

One time Elmer went to Bluffton to buy a new truck and the best buy they had was a red one. The salesman was insistent that he buy it and he told them, "I have a red-headed wife, four red-headed kids, and a red dog—now you want me to buy a red truck?" He came home driving a red truck. I think he loved it too because he drove it until the floor was all rotted out. I told him if he didn't get rid of it he would soon be running along on the ground trying to keep up with it.

Our living room held a lot of joy again this year. All the families came Christmas Eve and spent the night. It is still easy to get the little ones to bed. As usual Jim was the first one up and as usual woke all the little ones, and as usual was threatened with annihilation!

Christmas Day was spent resting and the evening was spent with Mom and Dad. They enjoy their little home so much. They are cozy and warm and no longer have to brave the elements to milk cows and feed chickens. They have earned this happiness and much more.

We are thankful for all these blessings and for our six dear grandchildren. Now we are fifteen in number!

1964

This has been a great year for Jim. He bought his first car, a blue Chevrolet that had belonged to Marvin and Gladys Putterbaugh. During the summer Linda and the boys were visiting us. Jim was taking a bath after having washed his car. A sudden storm came up and he yelled for somebody to roll up his car windows, but by that time the hailstones were so large nobody would venture out. When it was all over he had the job of scooping hailstones. I have never before or since seen such golf ball-sized chunks of ice! We gathered some of them and kept them in the freezer for a long time. A lot of windows downtown were knocked out and the boys were busy at repairs in several places.

Along with June came another grandson! Don and Linda gave us Patrick Donavon. As soon as he was home from the hospital the families packed up the kids and food and we were on our way to Indianapolis to see him. We made Linda take it easy. The little ones spent most of the day playing in the swimming pool Don had bought for his sons. It was such a warm, beautiful day, but any day is warm and beautiful when you have a new grandchild! They are growing so fast. Mitchie and Janelle are in first grade already!

Early this spring our town acquired two new doctors. We were pretty much adrift after Dr. Woods died and had to go out of town for a doctor. Our family has been very fortunate to have good health, but it is comforting to know doctors are near if you need them. The time came in December when we were very thankful they were near. Elmer, they found, had suffered heart damage and until further tests they were unable to tell whether the damage was recent or from an earlier time. His blood pressure was very high and they wanted to hospitalize him but he promised to obey all the rules if they would allow him to stay home. That put an end to our New Year's fun but our friends went to Guolocks and stood in line for two hours. It also put a strain on Christmas. The kids didn't stay all night and we sure missed them! Each family was allowed to come on Christmas day and stay only for a short time.

The scars on Elmer's heart proved to be old ones, but he will be on blood pressure medicine from now on. I know he works too hard, but I guess he has a built-in mechanism that isn't satisfied with anything less than "full speed ahead." It is just as hard for him to slow down as it is for me to speed up. When we lived in Markle our neighbor, Jack Adams, asked me once if Elmer ever wore out a pair of shoes. I said, "Why do you ask?" He replied, "His feet never touch the ground, so I don't know how he can wear out a pair of shoes!"

His blood pressure led to an awful argument. I begged him to slow down on account of it but he argued that he didn't have high blood pressure because he took medicine to keep it down! We may both be right but I know I'm the "rightest"!

This Christmas I experienced many emotions. Worry and uncertainty on one hand and joy and pride of possession on the other. The worry about my husband's health gnawed at my insides day and night. If I did not have a Heavenly Father to go to I don't know what I would have done. He comforts me and whatever tomorrow brings I know He will be with me. My joy and pride in my family gives me a lot to look forward to. I enjoy seeing our grandchildren well taken care of. Life has been good and whatever the future holds I know it will be according to the Plan.

1965

This has been a bad year for many people. On Palm Sunday a terrible tornado swept through southeast of Bluffton and many people were left homeless. The storm was terrible in our area too but Elmer slept right through it. When he went to awaken Jim to get ready for school Jim said, "There won't be any school today!" Elmer said, "What do you mean, no school?" "Half of Wells County blew away last night, Dad, and there won't be any school!" I was completely ignorant of the fact too, for I was in Lutheran Hospital recovering from surgery. I knew there was a bad storm but never dreamed of the extent of the damage!

When I came home the next week I stayed with Kirby and Shirley because we were still without lights and heat.

One of the places Elmer was called to was Jake and Enzie Tarr. Jake was our next-door neighbor when we lived in our first home. Their house was so beaten up and the structure was so weakened they decided to build a new house. One of the unheard-of things that took place was that the roof was lifted and the drapes were sucked outside and the roof set back down!

Jim graduated in May and the family gathered for a nice party, as we had for the other three. He still likes Sandy so we invited her and her family, which made Jim very happy.

Jim traded his car for a new GTO. We were a little skeptical at his doing it, but knew Uncle Sam has his eye on him. He enjoys it very much and is very proud of it.

Kirby and Shirley have bought a home in the country. Now Byron and Juli have a nice yard to play in. Our town isn't very large, but I know from experience it is much easier to raise children in the country. Jim was only five when we left town and I gave up my police action. In town you either have a yardful of kids or are calling and running all over town trying to find your own! Jim spent hours playing under the maple tree outside the kitchen window, building roads, taking his kittens for rides in his army trucks, or sitting in the tree, with his blanket wrapped around him, just taking in the sights! One day I pointed out to his dad that I was never going to get grass to grow in the spot where the "army" was building roads! His answer was beautiful—"Well, maybe when we can't raise boys anymore, we can raise grass!"

I recall another "army encampment" on the hill beyond our garden when we lived in Markle. It was during the war and all the boys were "soldiers." Jerry and his friends hauled a lot of big boxes from downtown and built "barracks" all over the hill. They dug holes and set up quite an encampment. It looked like the dickens but they were having fun and I knew where they were. They were in plain view from my kitchen window. I was busy baking pies one day and missed a good show, for after they had cooked their mess they had gone on maneuvers over on the hill behind Vaughn and Hilda's house. They looked back to the "base" and it was going up in flames! They chopped dirt to throw on it and someone ran over to Mary Buroff's house and grabbed her garden hose. The combination of chopping and watering finally put the fire out, and about three years later I found out that someone in the heat of excitement had chopped the garden hose in two! If I recall correctly some of Lucille Ormsby's and Josephine Baker's good blankets went up in smoke along with the cardboard cartons! It wasn't half as much fun cleaning it all up as it was to build it. Later on they used Grandpa's trailer as a base hospital. One day Jerry came in with a peculiar odor about him. I found out he had been shot in the leg and his buddies hauled him into the trailer and rubbed his leg with Grandpa's wine! I guess it healed him. Anyway he came through without a limp!

Kirby and Shirley have a nice home with a big barn. I know Kirby will want a horse now that he has a place for one. Jean kept the little ones on moving day and Linda and I helped with the settling in. It was so much fun helping them.

Later on in the summer Don and Linda moved to Cincinnati. They seemed so far away and I get so anxious to see them! Soon after the move Jim, Sandy, Elmer and I went to see them. They lived on Miami Avenue. We found Miami Avenue but no Don and Linda! We drove and drove and everyone was ready to give up and come home except me. I insisted they stop at the police station and I inquired there. I was so upset and about to leave when an officer said, "There's a Miami Avenue in Terris Park, you might inquire there." The river divided the two places but we soon found them. That was once when my perseverance paid off.

Sandy has become very much a part of Jim's life and he asked if he might bring her to our house for dinner. Of course he could! The day arrived and Jim asked what we were going to have to eat. When I mentioned corn-on-the-cob he said, "Oh, no." I asked why and he said, "Because Dad eats it like he's playing a mouth harp!" I told Elmer to go easy on the corn-eating and all went well! Neither of the kids ate enough to nourish a canary! I remember the feelings I had the first time I visited Elmer's family. I could hardly eat because I knew they were taking stock of "Elmer's girl"! I found out later that Elmer was so embarrassed because his dad poured his coffee in his saucer to cool! It is so funny now, just as I know their first meal will be to Jim and Sandy someday.

At Christmas time they were all with us again. Jim dressed up like Santa and the little ones were so surprised they hardly moved. Later Court said he didn't think it was the real one because his mouth didn't move when he talked! Santa's helpers carried in a new colored TV for Grandma and was she ever surprised!

The magic of Christmas makes it so hard for the little ones to fall asleep on Christmas Eve but after numerous drinks and trips to the bathroom they all settled down. At five o'clock they were all awakened by—guess who? I pity him when he has a family of his own. Somebody is going to get even—namely Linda Gay, Norma Jean and Shirley Mae!

We spent the evening with Mom and Dad. Mom had a nice supper. Cloyd and Marjorie and their family were there too. Mom is seventy-eight and Dad is eighty-two! I am so thankful they can be together in their own home. They love their little house. Dad walks downtown every day and Mom has good neighbors she visits with. I wish Dorothy and Mary could live closer, but Dorothy and Darwin get down pretty often from Alvordton, Ohio. Mary and Raymond come once a year from Memphis but they are good to write every week, which gives the folks something to look forward to.

There is much to be thankful for as this season ends and we think about the New Year, which is just around the corner.

1966

This year started out fine. Don was not happy with his job and with city living and went for an interview with Common Wealth in Jackson, Michigan. He got the job and soon started working there. It was a long ways from Cincinnati, but he went home every weekend. I knew Linda would be lonely on her birthday, and Elmer suggested I go spend some time with her. I invited Josephine to go with me to wish her a happy birthday. The night we got there Don called and had found a house that he loved but hesitated to do anything until Linda could see it. We were all excited but Linda didn't know how she could go so far with three little boys. I came up with the plan that I would stay with the boys and she and Josephine could drive to Fort Wayne where she could catch a train for Jackson. After a lot of hustling around, the two and the brown Plymouth disappeared over the hill and I was a stand-in mother to three little boys! Mitch and Pat didn't give me any trouble, but that Court was like a greased icicle—when I thought I had him well in hand he melted down and was gone again! He knew everybody in the neighborhood and I spent half my time leaving baby Pat alone while I chased him down! I finally spanked his butt and made him stay in bed for half a day. He was just as surprised as I was but drastic circumstances called for drastic measures. We have since forgiven each other.

Don and Linda came home thrilled to death. They had bought a big old house and forty acres of land! I could hardly wait to see it. I drove to Napoleon and was there when the van came with their furniture. The house was so much like ours in Markle that I felt right at home. I was glad I went, for Linda was glad for the help. The next Saturday Jerry's, Kirby's, Jim and Elmer came and stayed all night. We slept on the floor after the beds were filled.

The little boys were so happy with the big yard and the hill back of the house. Now they have a place to play in the wide-open spaces and there is plenty of room—even for Courtney!

Jim had been such an avid fan of Gomer Pyle that I blame Gomer for what happened next in our lives. Dave Bell, Nick Chaney, Gary Netherland and Jim, old buddies in school, decided they wanted to join the Marines! I didn't think I could bear having another son join the service, but the four left in July and his sweet boyish face will be imprinted on my heart forever. From what I had seen of Vietnam on TV, they were in for no picnic! He was our last one to leave home and the house was so empty without him. The other children were so wonderful and tried to ease our pain with frequent visits.

We had visited Bill and Margaret Hahn's lake cottage and it brought alive Elmer's latent desire for a lake cottage. It did us a world of good to get out of the house and look at every cottage for sale in northern Indiana. For years Elmer had saved leftovers, saying, "That's for our lake cottage someday." We had lost it all in the fire when the shop burned. We found a place within our means on beautiful Lake George. The cottage wasn't too great, but the setting was beautiful. The cottage was cramped for our family, but we knew that in time we could remedy that. We had a speedboat that the young ones enjoyed and a fishing boat that we enjoyed. It was so relaxing to sit in the boat with a baited hook dangling over the edge and feel the wind in our hair and the gentle rocking of the boat lulling us into forgetfulness for a little while!

Not long after Jim was in San Diego, Margaret, Melba, Kirby and I took Sandy to California where she and Jim were married in a beautiful little chapel on the base. Captain Pierto preformed the ceremony and was so nice to us while we were there.

When the first astronauts landed I was watching TV and the chaplain who gave thanks for their safe return was none other than Captain Pierto!

Sandy stayed with her cousin who lived near the base, but Jim never got any leave so in about a week a very homesick girl flew home.

I would love to take a more leisurely trip with Kirby. He stops at all the gift shops and places of interest. We stopped at the Petrified Forest and saw part of the Grand Canyon. He missed his Shirley and everywhere we stopped he said, "I wish Shirley could see this!" I am sure sometime she will. Melba stubbed her toe and picked up a cactus thorn on the way home. I would love to see California again at a more leisurely pace with Elmer. I know he would enjoy it. Maybe someday—?

We spent a lot of time at our cottage. In any experience there is always a time that is recalled with pure joy! I always recall one time that probably seemed insignificant to everyone except myself. It was an early autumn day when Jean and Shirley and the four little ones came to the cottage where I had stayed to make curtains. Jeff and Byron went swimming but Juli, Janelle and I went fishing. Juli caught the first fish and the veteran fisherman sat about telling Janelle just how to catch a fish! Janelle resented the advice because she was much older and her seniority should have entitled her to catch the first one! Grandma had a ball and enjoyed herself immensely!

The part that I hold dear was the moonlit night—a light mist veiled the moon and its beams wrapped the earth in splendor. We built a fire in the backyard and roasted hot dogs and made "S'mores." A s'more is a treat I first heard of as assistant leader of the Girl Scouts. They got their name because of the fact that if you ate one you just had to have "S'more."

We sat around the fire for a long time just talking and listening to night sounds. There was no traffic, no interruptions of any kind—just this day, this time, this moment when I felt suspended somewhere between Heaven and earth, insulated against the worry of war and all the other troubles Man heaps upon himself!

When Christmas came we were all together again! Along with Christmas we also had a shower for Jim and Sandy. My heart was full of conflicting emotions. The fear of the future was almost greater than my happiness, yet there was so much to be thankful for. I know I must always trust in God and I do, but often fear for what He has in store for me. The hardest words to say are, "Thy will be done," and truly mean them.

Soon after the holidays Jim went to North Carolina. A man had come home instead of our boy who had left in July. When we saw him in California we could not believe our eyes and wouldn't have known him if Captain Pierto hadn't said, "Here he is, Mother!" Kirby and I were sick. He was the skinniest, saddest-looking piece of humanity I ever saw! I wanted our boys to become men but I prefer a slower process!

As I disassembled the Christmas tree and put away all the trimmings my heart was sad. Would we see our family together again next year?

1967

*E*arly this year I started working at the coil factory in Huntington. That week we had a terrible ice storm and the power was off. We cooked in and kept warm by our fireplace. Elmer slept on the davenport and I sacked out in the recliner. It was not bad except for taking a bath in a cup of water. That bath again! My job was good for me as I was too tired to think when night came. One of my dear friends since childhood worked with me, dear Mildred! We have shared so much. We also worked together at General Electric nearly forty years ago and had many memories to relive. We stayed with her aunt and shared a room. Her sister and three other girls stayed there too. One night we got to talking about Walgreen's chocolate sodas and decided we just had to have one, so we coaxed Gladys and Ethela Truby to go with us. We rolled our pajama legs up, put on our coats, and rode the streetcar up town and had our chocolate sodas!

We had our own shelf in the icebox and our prunes kept disappearing. One girl left for work later than we did so we had a good idea where our prunes were going! At noon we often bought a box lunch for twenty-five cents and ate in the little park close to the fac-

157

tory. Sometimes we took the streetcar to a little restaurant beside the Broadway Theater where we enjoyed our first "Sloppy Joe" sandwiches. Across the street was a doughnut shop where we bought the first glazed doughnuts I ever ate, and ate, and ate! I guess that's why our shelf was so tempting. We thought of our stomachs first and the other girl spent her money for clothes and ate our prunes!

Anyway, here we were working together again. Her five children and my four were all grown so we had a lot to share. Besides that we were both grandmothers and they have even more to talk about than mothers.

Jim went to North Carolina and his letters to Mom and Dad were fewer. Sandy shared hers with us so we heard from him indirectly.

Now he has another reason to come home! Angela Sue Kay came to us and we are grandparents for the eighth time! She is a dear little girl and looks just like her Daddy. Sandy and Angie are living with Bill and Margaret until Jim comes home. There are dark days ahead for Sandy, for we feel sure Jim will be sent to Vietnam. She has her little girl to keep her busy and I hope the time goes quickly! He had a short leave and came home again and upon his return was sent to California. He had a little more free time and was able to visit with Nick and Sue. He called one night when Sandy was here and said Nick and Sue invited her to come stay with them until the boys shipped out. She thought there was no way she could go. I had a little secret cache I had been saving for a new dining room table and chairs but felt it was much more important that Jim, Sandy and their baby have time together than that we have new furniture.

Angie was so tiny and I felt terrible seeing Sandy fly away with her! She stayed until Jim was sent to Vietnam and the worst time was upon us!

We tried to create many things to occupy our time. We went to Don and Linda's as often as we could. We went to the cottage on Friday night and on to Jackson the next day, back to Indiana on Sunday and back to Markle on Monday morning.

Our little ones are growing up too fast:

Mitchell is ten;

Janelle is nine;

Jeffrey is eight;

Byron is seven;

Courtney is seven;

Juli is four;

Patrick is three;

Angela hasn't had a birthday yet.

Christmas in the house was a gay affair for the sake of the little ones but Christmas in the heart was very sad. The news from Vietnam was very distressing and it seemed fear stalked my every step. We sent many packages to Jim so he would remember there was something to live for—something to come home to.

I have found much comfort working in my flowers and garden. There is something so relaxing about it and feeling close to my maker when I stir the brown earth and plant seeds. Scientists can perfect a better strain of corn or beans but it takes that special spark of something to awaken the energy that brings it to life and fruition. Unfortunately, the same spark is alive in weed seeds and my garden suffered from neglect. When the morning was bright and cool I was on my way to a hot, smelly, old factory where my hands were covered with grease and compound all day! When the weather was nice I stood at the open door during break looking at the sun and sky and called myself a fool. I'm afraid my retirement will come soon!

I think of all the beautiful flowers and trees and birds and how well they cooperate. I would certainly never question the wisdom of God, but I often wonder if, after He created the universe and all the beautiful things in it, He wouldn't have saved Himself a lot of trouble if He had just forgotten Adam and Eve!

My hope is that somewhere along the grisly path my Marine walks, a little flower grows!

1968

This is truly a Christmas to be thankful! Our whole family gathered once more around the Christmas tree and there was another angel! Joni Lynn was born in February on the same day Sandy left for Hawaii to be with Jim on R & R. Shirley, Byron, Juli and I took her to the airport after which I went to K-Mart to pick up a few things. I asked Shirley if she felt all right and she said she was fine. We stopped at Atz's for lunch and when she turned down an ice cream sundae, I knew it was time to get her home. That evening they dropped Byron off to stay with us. (Juli stayed with Ed and Helen.) Then they were off to the hospital where our fourth granddaughter was born.

It was fun having a hungry little boy get off the school bus to drink hot chocolate and eat peanut-butter sandwiches again.

When Shirley and Joni came home, I went over in case the baby needed attention during the night. I slept right through the night and Shirley took care of the baby herself! When Byron was born I went the next day to see my new grandson and his mother. She was in need of having the head of her bed raised and before I could get off the chair and around the bed she had jumped out and cranked it up herself! Back in my productive days one was forced to say in bed for nine days, and not lie with one's arms over one's head! Juli was born while I was in the hospital with Mom after her gallbladder surgery.

When Margaret called me and said Sandy was in the hospital and would I please come up, my teeth chattered all the way to Bluffton.

When Mitchell was born it was supposed to be a surprise but Linda came home that morning to do her ironing and the surprise fell by the wayside. I'll never forget the look on Don's face when he arrived. His eyes were so big the whites shone all around them!

After they were gone I got dinner but neither of us could eat—who can when a miracle is about to happen? In just a few hours we gained the distinguished titles of "Grandpa and Grandma!" We raced to Fort Wayne to see our first grandchild. Mitchell Delayne was so tiny! The first thing I saw was the dimple in his chin, just like Grandfather's and Great-Grandfather's!

Janelle's birth was not the surprise it was supposed to be either. At about 6:00 on a Tuesday morning, Dorothy called me and said, "I think our kids think they are pulling something over on us. I just saw them sail around the corner and where else would they be going except to the hospital?"

I eyed the three bushels of peaches on the back porch and hoped it was a girl. The day before, Jean and I had bought them intending to can them the next day. When she left that night I said, "It would be just like you to go to the hospital tonight and leave me stuck with all these peaches!" She said, "If I do and it's a girl, I'll name her 'Alfreda'." So, all day I canned peaches with my eyes glued to the road for some sign of Jerry, but he didn't come that day or the next! On Thursday he called and asked if I would come to the hospital. When I arrived I found him draped over a chair in the waiting room sound asleep! I sat beside Jean waiting and hoping.

Finally, the next day a little girl made her appearance—and her name? Alfreda Janelle! I thought "Peaches" would have been a nice name too!

Jeffrey Allyn didn't take so long. His grandpa said it was because he was a boy—it's girls and women you have to wait on all the time!

Courtney was born in Lafayette and Patrick in Indianapolis, and Grandmother knew nothing about it 'til it was all over! That's the most painless way of becoming a grandmother!

We had a nice yard and garden this year and on this never-to-be-forgotten day of June 22nd I was out mowing the yard for thanks be to God our Jim would be home this day! It was such a relief and joy that the tears flowed often. I can endure a tearless sadness but joy streams from my eyes, and flying around on my lawn mower was a fine time to enjoy my world!

Jerry and Kirby were busy spraying "Welcome Home" on one of my good white sheets when Jim, Sandy and little Angela came flying in the driveway! Bill, Margaret, Melba, Jerry and Kirby with their families were here to greet him. Don and Linda and the boys came in the afternoon. Our dear friend Josephine came and her tears nearly broke my composure. It always distressed my children so much to see me cry that I have always tried to suppress my feelings as much as possible. When Elmer's mother died, our six-year-old Jerry said, "You won't cry will you, Mama?" It distressed the little fellow so much that I did my very best! I had missed her so much and the lovely talks we used to have! She was so wonderful to me. Sometime after she was gone I had a dream. In it we sat talking while we shelled beans. When I arose next morning the awful gnawing ache on my insides was gone, and I guess that was when I truly gave her up to a better life while I must live out my own without her. She was the first one of our close family circle to leave and it was hard to bear!

The little ones felt bad because their uncle Jim didn't chase them and play with them like he had before, but Jim came home a man with responsibilities and our little boy was no more!

Sandy rented a trailer in Bluffton where they lived for a month. Then Joyce and Ron Green bought Ruth Ratliff's house and Jim and Sandy rented the little brown house where Jean and Jerry started their lives together.

This year our last child gathered his family around his own Christmas tree.

Everybody came home Christmas Eve loaded down with packages and all were curious about the huge box in the corner with all their names on it. It held card tables and chairs for each family. All the fun of Christmas comes in the anticipation I see on all their faces. Sometime before the big day the grandchildren (sometimes the big ones too) have a turn at crawling around under the tree exploring and guessing.

This was the year for everybody to get even with Jim and I heard the girls discussing what time they were going to awaken Angie! When they got up, there sat Jim holding his little girl in his arms! After the little ones were asleep was when the big ones visited and relaxed. The result is always the same. The grandchildren arise ready to go and the poor, tired parents can hardly open their eyes. I smile to myself thinking that history is repeating itself!

After a good breakfast everyone left to make other grandparents happy. They all returned in the evening and enjoyed chicken soup and oyster stew with us.

So ends 1968 with me at home, having quit my job at Square D.

1969

*O*nce again it is the time in between and we reminisce over the year just past. A new one will soon be here.

It seems like only yesterday, but a whole year has passed since our party with Guy and Edna as hosts. It was a very cold night but we made it to the Show Lounge for dinner and back to Guy and Edna's for an evening of fun and ushering in the New Year to the music of Guy Lombardo. We look forward to these parties as a time of renewing old acquaintances and to the fact that our families are all grown and we can kick up our heels a little (if you can call going out to eat at a nice place and staying out until after midnight "kicking up your heels"). We do enjoy these times with friends of many, many years. Carl and Elmer grew up together and one time Roscoe, Helen, Elmer and I went to Boehmer to a Children's Meeting where we were introduced to Carl's friend Mary. Helen and I sort of lost her in the crowd and tried to determine which one was her. Later Mary told me that she saw us looking at her and thought we were talking about her and she didn't like us very well! We became close friends and have remained so ever since. Mildred and I have been good friends for years but not as long as

Helen and I. We were classmates in school and stuck together like glue. Her telephone number was 94-6r and mine was 86-2B. My mother used to say, "Can't you girls get all your talking done in school without talking two hours every night?" The world was new and we had to share our discoveries!

Edna was Mildred's bothersome little sister for years but she finally matured enough that she was accepted into the "elite" crowd! Guy and Carl are practically newcomers but fit in just fine!

Earlier this year we took a nice trip to Nova Scotia with Ted and Josephine. We saw the "rockbound coasts of Maine," and rode on a boat across the Bay of Fundy from Maine to Digby. It was a beautiful trip. The weather in Nova Scotia was so nice and the water was so blue! I counted many lakes and it seemed strange there were few cottages on them. Ted said the people there saw so much water a lake didn't hold any thrills for them. Indiana lakes are so crowded it's hard to find a place to squeeze in another cottage.

We visited a fish processing plant and many other places, and came home via Niagara Falls. I was enthralled with the beautiful lupines in such a range of colors they are hard to describe. They grew everywhere and I wanted to pick them all and bring them home!

Around Niagara Falls all the flowers were so beautiful because of the moisture in the air.

The most wonderful gift received this summer was a set of twins! They were born September 12th, just a few weeks after Jim and Sandy moved into their own home. They bought a little house that stands near the spot where I started Sunday School! The church was demolished when the new road was built, just as were some of the houses that stood in the way of "progress," one of which was saved by Jerry and Jean.

Angie stayed with us while Sandy was in the hospital. She is a sweet little girl and I enjoyed her. One day when Grandma was busy in her kitchen a little girl came and took her by the finger and led her to the bedroom hallway to show Grandma her "artwork." With Grandma's lipstick, she had decorated the walls, the baby bed, the chest of drawers and just about everything in between! She was so proud of her accomplishment and smilingly awaited her Grandma's approval! How can you possibly withhold it when innocent blue eyes are eagerly anticipating it?

Jim had looked forward to a son and when he came and glowingly announced the birth of little sisters I said, "Oh, Jim, you didn't get your boy!" He immediately came up with, "What's wrong with three little girls?"—nothing at all! Linda has three boys and she and Jim discussed trading a girl for a boy but I don't think either of them could decide which one they wanted to trade.

We were shocked and saddened with the sudden death of our dear friend, Fern Sills. She suffered a fatal heart attack November 22nd. We will miss her so much—we shared so many good times! We were Worthy Matrons of our Eastern Star Chapters the same year and Elmer and Ray were very active in their Masonic Lodge work. We enjoyed a nice trip through the south with them, except when Ray, Fern and I got sicker than dogs! I don't know why Elmer always manages to escape. Not only this time—but also on Guy and Edna's honeymoon when he was the only one who didn't get infested with a mess of chiggers!

Fern and I had many serious conversations, especially in these last years. She seemed to be constantly searching for answers and my hope is that she has found them in the safe haven that is our afterlife! Her life had been no picnic and through her own admission, she revealed that had she stayed with the father of her sons, life might not have had so many problems. Ray was a good friend and a reasonably good husband, but he batted zero as a stepfather! Both sons served in World War II. Rex, who had lived with his grandmother, was killed in an auto accident in Fort Wayne. Fern was devastated. Her sorrow seemed too deep for any words of comfort to reach, and my heart ached for her! Our wrongs rise up to haunt us in later years. It is so easy to take the wrong path and it is very important to give a lot of serious thought to every situation that requires a decision. My dear neighbor, Amanda Foust, whose wisdom I marveled at and envied, told me when I was a foundering, bubble-headed newlywed that no young married couple should be without the Marriage Bears in their lives. Their names are "Bear" and "Fore-Bear!" She said, "When you see your mate is very angry let him blow off steam and walk away. After a while he will cool off and you won't have said a lot of things you are sorry for!" What wonderful advice, but how hard to follow, and I didn't a lot of times. There have been times I wanted to run home to Mom, but I knew I would get no sympathy there. We have learned tolerance goes hand-in-hand with love and that without the former the latter is in danger of Big Trouble!

Christmas was very beautiful this year. A snowfall covered all the ugliness and the out-of-doors looked like the pictures you often see on calendars, or an inspired artist product.

Janelle gave up a shopping trip with Tammy to help Grandma. She said that being the oldest granddaughter, she felt it her duty! We put the final touches to the house, made beds to accommodate twenty-one people and got supper after which we cleared the dishes and settled down to wait the arrival of the rest of the family. It wasn't long before the old house was filled with laughter and gladness as we all greeted each other. Everyone enjoyed singing as we gathered around the organ, with Shirley furnishing the accompaniment. Even little Joni and Angie sang! The three-month-old twins just yawned and slept.

We love these times and will treasure them forever! The old house finally settled down for the night, which always seems not half long enough.

Guess who was the first one up? So far, the girls haven't been able to get even with Jim!

1970

The last night of last year started out in a funny situation. We were hosts of our New Year's party this year and were hurrying to get ready. Elmer locked himself out of the bathroom with the water running in the tub! We couldn't find the key and had visions of an overflowing tub as Elmer picked the lock standing in his birthday suit! We, as usual, had a good time with our friends. We went to Baer Field for dinner and came back here, played cards, talked and as usual greeted the New Year with Guy Lombardo. All were gone by two-thirty and two tired people fell into bed.

New Year's Day is such a nice time. Looking back over the old year we can assess our losses and gains and look to the new year when we will try to profit from our losses and add to our gains. Not necessarily in dollars and cents, but in the quality of our lives. The new year is a blank sheet and we look forward to what will be written there next year.

The new addition to the church was finished this year and I hope Elmer can relax a little! He takes his work very seriously and all during our trip to Nova Scotia I knew his mind was back home on the church project so intently that he didn't enjoy himself.

I know you have heard of "Dog Days"—well this has been a "Dog Year" for this family. We now have Harvey who was Jim's dog but who refused to stay home after he chewed up their lawn furniture and Jim gave him "obedience training" about four times. He kept running off and coming out here so now he is our dog!

Jeff named his birthday dog "Nipper" on his eleventh birthday. Jean and I went to Fort Wayne to bring him home. He was so cute! We stopped at Azar's in Waynedale to get a bite to eat when Nipper had an awfully smelly accident in the front seat. After cleaning up the mess we decided neither of us wanted pumpkin pie for desert!

Linus joined the Carl family and keeps Wiggles on his toes. Don gained a lot of attention once when he drove through Jackson on the way to the vet with Linus riding in the back of the truck. He is a St. Bernard and he is a *big* St. Bernard!

Mom had a heart attack in February. I worry about the future—Bill and Margaret's house burned February 13th. The drug store also caught fire and the boys were called to redo it also. They had this extra work and had a full schedule. Jim is on the fire department and has passed his life-saving tests. Their lives are very busy with their three girls. Their home is very small but they are making a good start by buying their own home. Now they all have homes of their own and we have always felt that was the way to go, and that paying rent was a waste of money.

Don and Linda are still working on their house and it will be lovely when it is finished. It is an old house with lots of character that isn't found in a new one.

Jerry and Jean have added a garage to their house. It has done much to visibly lower the three stories and ties them to the landscape.

Kirby and Shirley are taking a breather in their remodeling but will be back at it before long. The great thing is that all the children have a nice, safe place to play!

I spent a weekend with the boys while Don and Linda went on a canoe trip. We took a picnic one day and went to a nearby lake where the boys swam and had a good time while I caught up on my reading. On the way home the boys insisted we go to "Goose Lake" rock festival! *No Way!*

We celebrated our fortieth wedding anniversary September 20th by just starting out with no particular destination in mind. We went to Dunkirk and visited the glass factory, back to Portland for lunch and on to Amishville. For such a small place, I never enjoyed myself more. It was so appropriate that our anniversary would be spent by going back in memory to our early years together! When we came home we stopped to visit Grace and Wayne. Our last stop was with Ray where we had a cup of coffee and a lot of conversation. Ray is lonely and we try to see him often.

Our boys are playing ball now. Byron plays in Zanesville and Jeff at Markle. Mitch and Court play too, but we never get to see them. Mitchell and Jeff are Boy Scouts now and Court is a Weblo. We are pleased because Scouting is very good training for boys and girls too.

We made some new friends, Charles and Polly Bader, who stayed with us during Lay Witness Mission. Our visit was marred by news of the death of my dear Aunt Nora who died December 3rd. Uncle Howard, her brother, died December 27th. This new year will mean a lot of adjustment for their families and for Mom. She is the only one left of a family of two brothers and three sisters. My heart aches for her for she herself isn't well and to lose someone so close to her as Aunt Nora was a great shock. They were very close and phoned each other almost every day. Long ago when I was a kid, Dad and Uncle Jesse would imitate the two of them on the phone. This always sent us kids into spasms of laughter! Mom and Aunt Norma talked mostly of their ailments and Dad and Uncle Jesse made the most of it in their rendition!

I know Mom and Dad have some pleasant memories if they would only dwell on them. I guess when you are only sixty you shouldn't try to tell your parents of eighty-three and eighty-six how to live or what to think! I'm sure there is a lot of difference in how you see things on the other end of the years that divide us!

Our blessed children came again to make our Christmas bright. This year the grandsons slept on cots in the utility room, the granddaughters in their usual spot in our bedroom. It isn't easily recognizable, because in the preparation the two mattresses are placed side-by-side on the floor and nests made for the younger ones. The big girls, Janelle and Juli, sleep on the springs, which can't be as comfortable as the floor, but the higher position seems to appeal to them!

Grandpa and Grandma hide themselves in the den to grab what sleep there is between 1:30 and 4:45! A major change took place this year—the utility room gang routed everybody out and had the fun of displacing Jim!

We are so thankful for them all!

1971

This has been a short day. After such a nice New Year's party and the late hour, I stayed in bed until 11:15! Watched the Rose Bowl parade and Elmer watched football the rest of the day. I have called our families and wished them all a happy New Year.

We enjoyed a different sort of party this year. Mary surprised us with a lovely dinner at their house. There was much speculation about where we were spending the night, as we had instruction to bring our overnight bags. We found ourselves in a beautiful room at the Marriott Inn at Fort Wayne. The guys occupied one room and we gals another. We wanted to gab, so Mary put all the fellows together and we talked and played "dirty clubs" until 4:30, got up at 10:00 and ate breakfast at noon. I had a ball, but when we got home Elmer informed me that he was awake at six and laid there for two hours so as not to disturb anyone, and when he couldn't lie there one more minute he sneaked out and had explored the north end of Fort Wayne before anybody was up and he was nearly starved to death!

We looked forward to working on our cottage and by April had it all torn to pieces.

In the early part of May, Mom had her second heart attack. The following two months was a time of heartache and sorrow! I had always told myself that I would take care of them all their lives and it was terrible to find myself unable to do so! When Mary and Dorothy came home, Mom asked us to investigate the rest homes in the area. I was about worn out and Dr. Miller talked to Mom about going and Mom agreed. Dr. Miller said I might have been able to care for one of them but not both! We like Cooper's best and Mom said that would be fine and she was ready to go. I spent the last night with them in their own home and prayed to God to make the going easy for them! We packed the few things they were allowed to take the night before and it looked like a sorry little pile to me. There was no rest for me the remainder of the night and I didn't think I could survive the blow of their last goodbye to the little green house they were so proud of and loved so much! Marjorie came just as we were ready to leave and it helped a lot to have her there. Mom was a good patient but knew instinctively how sick and worried I was. She kept telling me, "They are all so good and kind to us here and I want you to stop your worrying! Everything is all right with me because someone is taking care of me!" Dad was another story—he didn't like the food or anything else about the place! He said there wasn't anybody there to talk to but old, sick people! He ran away and they had to restrain him for his own good. As soon as I got there he begged me to get him out of there. There was no way to make him understand why I couldn't and the pleading in his eyes nearly was my undoing! There were very few times in my life that I disobeyed him and to do it now when he needed me so badly made me feel like an ogre towering over this helpless creature who had always worked so hard to feed me and clothe me. I went to see them often and came away sick at heart. I felt so helpless on one hand and guilty on the other that I wasn't with Elmer to help him on the lake cottage. I knew he needed me, but there was no way I could abandon them! God mercifully took Mom home on July 9th. I know that she has found joy in her reunion with Aunt Nora and Uncle Howard! I am so thankful that Dad could follow her soon! On July 18th his long life of eighty-eight years was over and they rest side-by-side in our little cemetery on the banks of the Wabash. I don't think of them as being there but as being in a world where there is no worry! May I always cherish the memory of the good times and be forgetful of the times of frustration.

Jean lost her father on July 17th and her brother-in-law on the 8th of July. Shirley lost her Aunt Ruth also.

At the end of the summer the cottage was all enclosed but there was still much to be done.

All spent Christmas Eve with us except Don and Linda. They came the next day and were here Christmas night. We feel blessed, indeed when we are privileged to all be together this time of year! Of course a lot of my thoughts were with Mom and Dad. I missed them so much and remembered the dream I had after Elmer's mother was gone and asked God to comfort me as He had then. This will probably sound eerie to some people, but I feel my dear family should know this and remember it. I *did* have a dream—a most beautiful one, and after it was over I was comforted and able to live without the awful hunger in my insides! I lay in a field of golden, ripe grain and the field was dome-shaped. In the distance I could see the tops of green pine trees on the horizon. All was very peaceful and quiet, but I felt a little chilly. Then the most wonderful thing happened and I wasn't afraid. Someone drew a cover over me and it was made of a substance not found in this world! It was white as a cloud and downy soft! Then I saw the hands holding it and they were my mother's hands! All I saw were her hands but there was no mistaking them!

After Mom was gone Dad wanted to go so badly and cried as we four sisters gathered around his bed. He asked, "Why can't I go too?" I told him he must pray to God to take him and he said, "You pray!" and I did ending with the beautiful Lord's Prayer. At the finish he said, "How does that go now?" and with our help he uttered a few words. Why, oh why, did he try to bear life's burdens all alone when help was only a prayer away! His life was very hard. School wasn't compulsory when he was young and he didn't like to go, so he didn't. Every penny he made was made the hard way. He worried about everything so much. I appreciated his concern for his four girls. He loved us and many times when I was small he took me on his lap and caressed my red curls. His hand was rough and callused, but I could hear his strong heartbeat under my ear and felt safe and happy. No matter now badly he felt he went to work! I remember one time when he worked on the railroad, for seven dollars a week, he could hardly walk his back hurt so bad. He wore Mom's corset to work and swore us all to secrecy! He didn't get sick pay, paid vacation or double overtime.

I am glad this year is over. I know time will heal my sad heart. I want to be happy again!

This year Elmer retired and turned the business over to the boys. I can't see any difference in our lives except that he is home all day, and that his health isn't any better. He keeps books for the jobs and does the estimating, phone answering, and whatever he can do in the shop. I am thankful for these things to keep him busy because he would be miserable with nothing to do. He is an avid baseball, football, basketball and pro golfing fan but only on TV. He loves to read and has many, many books. We spend all the time we can in good weather sitting in our rocking chairs out of doors in the evenings enjoying each other's company. Seems like we don't talk much any more because we know each other so well we know without words what the other is thinking! One time when we were down to the Gateway for supper, Joyce and Pam and their families were seated close to us just chatting up a storm. Joyce turned to us and said, "Are you guys mad at each other or something? You haven't said a word to each other since we sat down!"

Many years ago we had planned to travel after retirement but I'm afraid it isn't possible now. He always dreamed of seeing the redwood trees in California. You don't always get to fulfill your dreams in life, but we are grateful for the many wonderful places we have been on our travels via the travelogues sitting in a soft seat in the theater at the schoolhouse in Bluffton!

We spend many hours in reminiscences and trying to remember, "What's-his-name's" name!

A long time ago I wrote a few lines never dreaming I would be living them soon!

Getting Old

The joys of growing old
Are the memories stored away
And you count them like rare jewels
Sometimes when you say,
"Do you remember?" "Yes, I do!"
As the moments go flying by
Recollections bring forth laughter
But sometimes you cry!

1972

I was glad to hang a new calendar on the wall. I don't know why because time goes too fast anyway! I guess I look forward to the new year as being better than the old one.

We started early as we could on the cottage but on March 27th Elmer went to the hospital for double hernia surgery. On the fourth day, which was a Sunday, I was getting ready to go see him when he called and said, "Come and get me!" It sounded like a cry of desperation and my first thought was that he was out of his head. I said, "What are you doing out of bed?" He convinced me the doctor had released him. On the way home he looked at everything as though he had been gone a month instead of four days and said, "Well, I guess everything looks about the same!" That's the first time he has ever been out of circulation that long and I guess four days in the hospital would drag on for a guy like him! He got along very well but had to take it easy for a while. We spent a lot of time at the cottage where he could putter around and do what he felt like doing. In June I had a gallbladder attack and on September 25th went in for surgery. Got along fine but couldn't hoe or pull weeds for a while. Shirley's mother suffers with the same trouble and I can't convince her how simple it is to have it out. Don's mother was treated for uterine cancer this summer. Jean's mother hasn't fully recovered from her automobile accident but she and Mildred (Carl's sister) flew to California to visit with Molly. I was so glad she could go. I know she misses Carl dreadfully, but she is very brave. I guess we are all falling apart at the seams. Harvey and Nipper both got their seams split on the road this summer. It is so hard for a child to lose a pet! I remember when Jim was small we had a dog named "Inky" that he loved very much. He got cross (the dog) and bit a few people and we had to get rid of him (the dog). A mother dog had come from somewhere and had pups under the house. I think it was a case of the "chickens coming home to roost" because a lot of the pups looked like Inky. Ruth Ratliff had a cat she asked me to take to the pound too, so Jim and I started to Fort Wayne with six dogs in the car and a cat in a covered basket in the trunk! Jim sat in the back seat with the pups and when we got just north of Zanesville announced that the cat was reaching her paw up beside him! I thought, "Heavens to Betsy, what if that cat squeezes its way in here with all these dogs?" We arrived at the pound and I felt terrible. Faithful little Inky sat close beside me all the way as if sensing danger. I felt like a traitor and asked the attendant not to let Jim know what he was going to do with them. I couldn't get Inky out of the car and I almost brought him back home. Finally Jim coaxed him out and the man said, "We will put these two in here because we have to get the fleas off of them before we put them in with the other dogs." In my heart I thanked him because I didn't want Jim to feel as bad as I did!

Kirby always loved animals too, but we felt the kids were safer not having a pet in town. One day he came home with a mutt on a long leash and carrying a box of dog food in his arms. He begged to keep the dog but we felt that if we had a dog it should be a housedog and this monster was no housedog. Elmer promised him if he would take it back he would buy him a nice puppy for his birthday. I'll never forget the sweet, curly-headed, sad-faced little boy with that dog on an eight- or ten-foot leash, his face tearstained and his chubby arms clutching the bag of dog food as he solemnly began the return trip. True to his promise, when Kirby's birthday came, his daddy brought him a little black toy manchester. The mutt was soon forgotten. After much deliberation over what to name it, Elmer said, "I think Kirby should name it since it is his dog!" He chose to call her "Cindy" which was short for "Cinders."

Bill and Margaret sold their cottage and bought a camper. I must confess that I don't get as big a thrill out of our cottage as I did when it was a leaky old shack!

I spent a lot of time this summer making things for our Christmas bazaar at church, and gifts for the family. It was a nice way to recover from surgery.

We had a nice Christmas with all the families here. We count our blessings every year, for we know that when the children are older we may not be so fortunate. Joni and Angie couldn't get to sleep and made frequent trips to where Grandma had a dish of big pretzels. In the morning the dish was empty and we poured salt out of their bed!

It is always such a sad sight after the festivities are over to see the naked little tree wondering where all the fun went! I like my new artificial tree, but the boys gave me a hard time about it. Their wives say they are spoiled and maybe they are. Jim says the tree just doesn't smell right—guess I'll have to find a pine-scented candle for him! I have a feeling that someday he will succumb to pressure when Sandy gets tired of sweeping up pine needles and digging resin out from under her fingernails!

Jerry's first tree in his own home was a dandy! It took up about a fourth of their living room. He bought it while Jean was at work to surprise her and he did! I stopped in to see it and there sat Jerry all sprawled out in a car with the most dejected look on his face. He said, "It didn't look that big when I bought it!" and there it stood, so tall that it bent over at the top and laid out about two feet across the ceiling! I laughed so hard I had to sit down. He said, "What am I going to do? I hate to cut it off and spoil the top!" I mentioned that he might cut two or three feet off the bottom. He said, "Well, I never thought of that!" My dear, dear son and his lesson in resourcefulness! You must learn that if what you have doesn't work you have to add to or take from it 'til it does work. A safety pin, a bobby pin, a stick, a piece of wire and string is something no household should be without. Loose screws in a storm door will stay put if you insert the short end of a toothpick in the hole and reinsert the screw. I know because our front storm door has been working six years with this minor repair!

The summer of the year Jim was born Elmer did some work at North Webster for Clarence and Hildreth Samson. We stayed in a nearby cottage and cooked on a two-burner oil stove that never got hot enough to boil water. I was so glad I had taken our percolator with us but lo-and-behold about the third morning the thing wouldn't work! I turned it upside down and removed a screw. There were the working parts, but they weren't working! I saw something between two screws that looked like a wire had melted. I looked around and all that was available was a piece of wire on the screen door. I confiscated a piece, wired the thing together, slapped on the bottom and PRESTO! We had hot coffee for breakfast! Would you believe I kept that thing going for three years before something more elusive happened to it?

It is rather deplorable that in this day and age everything you buy is bound with tape or wrapped in plastic. Nobody uses string anymore and kids are being cheated out of a cheap, educational toy! When I was a kid I loved to watch the clerk in the grocery store. He put everything in a reusable sack or wrapped it in reusable paper and tied a string around it. The string hung down from a little holder above his head and every time he yanked on it, it jumped up in the air and I was sure that some day it was going to fly out and land on his head! When my mother undid the packages she saved the string and we used it for many things. We kids made Jacob's ladders and chicken's feet. The wrapping paper served us too. Often we cut out pages and made books, which we then wrote in. Another fun thing was to fold it several times and cut out boys and girls and when we unfolded it had a row of boys and girls holding hands, or a row of animals holding the tail of the one in front of him in his mouth.

When we got something that came in a pasteboard box we were ecstatic! When the new Sears Roebuck catalogue came we inherited the old one—the glossy pages, that is, for the ones that could be crumpled into a soft handful were used for more important things. That used to be fun too. My sister or I would sit in the old two-holer and look at what was left of the catalogue. When we saw something we liked we would say, "I wish I had that!" When Mom heard us she would quote, "If wishes were horses, beggars could ride!" I couldn't quite understand that, because I didn't want a horse—I wanted a new dress!

We cut people and clothes out of the shiny pages and our favorite game was playing "Pilgrims." The dining room floor was the Atlantic Ocean. We loaded our cargo into the shoebox ship and cried bitter tears when we left our "Father Land," and chilled as the storms beset us on our journey across the dangerous expanse. When we landed our wild screams at the sight of Indians brought out mother from the kitchen to see what in the world was going on! When she saw we weren't killing each other she'd say, "Better get this mess cleaned up before your dad gets home!" We made the perilous trip so many times that our paper dolls were as worn out as the real travelers must have been!

That old house still stands just south of Jerry's and I'd like to go back there and just sit as long as I want to remember my childhood when life was so simple.

I guess I must be getting old to be recalling all these things, but it is interesting to think of the changes I have lived through. I should write a book!

We went to the Heidelberg in Huntington this year for our New Year's Eve party a day early this year. Ray and Emma spent New Year's Eve with us.

Early this year we invested in a housing addition in Michigan.

The greatest thing for our country this year was that the prisoners of war in Vietnam were released and brought home. It was a very, very poignant moment to witness as their arrival was shown on TV!

1973

This has been a good year with all of us in good health. The twins are four this year and Mitch is sixteen. He will soon be wanting a new car.

The boys have been busy this summer building the new mall east of town. It is quite an improvement to our town and I hope it is a success. It has a dry-goods store, hardware, and a grocery. Doctors Miller and Kinzer have done this in appreciation for what the town has done for them and I hope our town will patronize it and help make it a success. There are plenty of people to make it and Hill's Market both prosperous.

I can remember when our town boasted three groceries, Bender's, Lesh's and Redding's. Two of them, Bender's and Lesh's, also had dry-goods stores.

The joy of our young lives was to go to town on Saturday night. We had our baths in a galvanized tub late in the afternoon and were instructed to stay clean or we wouldn't get to go. Mom usually gave us each a slice of fresh, homemade bread spread with fresh homemade butter and sprinkled it with brown sugar. If the weather was warm we sat on the porch and enjoyed our treat while she took her bath and combed her long, dark hair.

After an early supper, Dad loaded the basket of eggs, the kerosene can and the cream can into the back of the buggy and we were away for a night on the town! If there was anything left after the trading was done sometimes we got to go to McCance's ice cream parlor. This didn't happen very often for seldom did the eggs and cream cover the cost of the groceries. Dad's favorite treat was enjoyed on Sunday morning. He often said, "If there's anything left, let's have a mess of beef steak for breakfast tomorrow morning!" Fresh meat had to be eaten soon because of the lack of refrigeration. Sometimes on a special occasion we had ice cream. Dad drove the mile and a half into town and raced home with it before it melted. The horse hadn't started normal breathing before it was all gone! I tried to make this pure joy last as long as I could but Dad would say, "Hurry up and eat that before it melts!" So I "hurried up and ate it before it melted" and often got a bad headache. It was worth it!

Sometimes we got a nickel to spend for candy and it took us longer to choose the kind than it does the U.S. Government to raise taxes! We often settled on gumdrops because they were so pretty. Jasper Slane learned to always include two black ones because we retired to the back of the store and fought over just one! Two other little girls, Enid and Olive Wilburn, had a good method I had never thought of. They sat on the steps at the back of the store like two ladies. Enid divided the candy by biting a piece in half and giving Olive the rest of it. I never knew whether Olive got her fair share or not!

Our town once had a cream, egg and poultry place where my friend Helen and I stopped once a week to weigh ourselves for want of something to do. The Blacksmith, which was run by my friend Mildred's father, was a place I loved to visit. I loved to watch him shoe a horse and was always amazed at how quietly the horse stood while Harmon drove nails into its feet! It wasn't 'til much later I learned the nail only went into the hoof. When he reached into the forge with his tongs and lifted out the metal it was red hot and the sweat poured off his brawny arms as he hammered it into shape on his anvil! He had a horseshoe court back of his shop where many men and boys gathered to relax and play horseshoes.

We had two barbershops and in one of them I had my curls cut off. My Dad had a fit because Mom let me get my hair "bobbed," but all the other girls were doing it, so it was much like girls today wanting to get their ears pierced. It is to show the world we are growing up, just like the fight with long underwear was. You kids will never know what a fight for independence that war was! The "union suit" was a heavy cotton, fleece-lined suit of armor with long sleeves and legs. They buttoned down the front and had a trap door in the back that you unbuttoned and lowered to attend to nature's recurring signals! When three-quarter-length socks and above-the-knee dresses came into style I wasn't about to go to school with bulky, long underwear under my stockings. I wanted blue knees in freezing weather like the other girls had! When I got to school I rolled the hateful things up and pinned them with safety pins I had confiscated from my baby sister's wardrobe. I had awfully enlarged knees but my full skirt covered them!

My girl friend's big sister Hazel, after a terrible argument about this very thing one Saturday, seized the scissors, rushed upstairs, grabbed a pair of the hateful things and cut the legs off. Unfortunately for her, in her haste she had cut the legs off her mother's "longies" instead of her own!

In our town we had a beautiful store knows as "Burneaus." It was a dry goods and millinery store. It had a low sink and a pump in the middle of it and we kids always had to have a drink out of the tin cup that everybody else in town drank from! What would Blackburn say about that, I wonder!

Beside the bank was a shoe repair shop run by Billy Michael, who was the father of Martha. She became a schoolteacher and was

Jerry's teacher. She and I became good friends through our association in Eastern Star.

Al Stauffer's store was a men's clothing store where the men gathered to go over the affairs of the day and to purchase their clothing. Al played in the Markle band for years and was an active member of the Masonic Lodge for as long as he lived.

There was a movie theater on the south side of the main street but I didn't get to go very often. I saw a "Hoot Gibson" movie there once and he became my teenage idol! He always got the bad guy and if he were alive today he could jump on any horse running at breakneck speed in the Kentucky Derby, unhampered by the weight of a gun belt, bullets, two heavy pistols and the coil of rope he carried in his hand! All this beautiful action took place without a sound except for the music Harry Youse pumped out of the player piano! You read what was happening underneath the picture!

Another wonderful thing happened on Wednesday night in the summer time—the band concert! If Dad wasn't too tired we sometimes got to go. If we didn't and the wind was just right we could hear the music from our yard.

Kelsey's butcher shop stood on part of the land that is now the town lot. A little picture gallery stood beside it and south of both was the hotel, which has since been moved west and now is a private home on the banks of the Wabash.

May and Youse owned a lumberyard which stood where the boat factory now is. Many of the beautiful old houses in our town were once logs hauled three or four at a time on horse-drawn wagons to the sawmill near the Erie railroad.

We had two grain elevators near the railroad and the Thomas Flour Mill, which stood beside the Wabash near the dam, and was run by waterpower for many years. Unfortunately the beautiful old landmark was set on fire and destroyed by vandals. Tragedy also overcame the old covered wooden bridge just east of own. It, too, was burned to the ground!

Our dear old school house is gone too. I recall such wonderful memories where I spent eight years of my life! I started at the Brickly school but after some officials went on a modernization kick, we were hauled into town.

Our parents were aghast that "They are hauling our kids clear into Markle!" This writer was privileged to ride the first school bus into town. Brickly school had closed and in my fourth grade my horizons were expanded to riding the one and a half mile rather than walking one half mile to school.

Earl Yoose, a brother of Grace who was one of three of our senior citizens to ride in Markle Wildcat parade as Grand Marshall, was our first bus driver. He drove his family's five-passenger sedan into which he crammed seven of us. Our number grew and he had to make other provisions. The larger car was a touring car with side curtains to make use of in case of rain. It also had two "jump-seats" which unfolded from the front seat of the car. We raced every day to get to ride in the jump seat. You couldn't see where you were going, but you could sure see where you'd been!

Many of we Oldsters are riding "jump-seats" again. We prefer to remember the past than to look into the future. Perhaps it's because there's so much more of it!

The teachers who both goaded us and inspired us were dedicated to their jobs. Nobody ever heard of such a thing as a teacher's strike!

Most of them are gone now but they are certainly not forgotten! I am always amazed when I stop to think of how they were able to take masses of raw material and turn out thinking machines!

Part of our school supplies included lunch pails, because there were no cafeterias. Neither were there gym classes, swimming pools, marching bands, computers, sex education, cross-county, or

"Hoosier Hysteria"! Yet, when we graduated we had learned the basic principles of becoming useful human beings. In my old-fashioned way I can't help wondering if the "quality" of education has somehow become diluted by the "quantity"!

When the paddle followed the hickory switch into oblivion, teachers were robbed of an ally in discipline. In the principal's office at Markle High School hung a big, long paddle! I never knew of it being used but it hung there as an emblem of authority and believe me, we respected it. I never in twelve years met a mean teacher, but I knew that if I didn't behave myself they could get that way! Not only that but I knew that when I got home my parents would get that way too!

In 1928 my parents bought a farm and I had to leave my friends. My last year was enjoyable too, because I soon made friends and had wonderful teachers. I graduated from Lafayette Central into the school of experience. I will say that I have learned much more in the latter, but learned the basics in the former!

Some of our citizens now resting in our beautiful cemetery have told me that when they were young many Indians lived near our town and enjoyed friendly relations with their white neighbors. In fact Elmer's great grandfather and mother met at an Indian dance west of town where Rockcreek empties into the Wabash. I have often regretted that I didn't delve farther into the town's history at that time but my children were small and I was a very busy person. For many years, half of an Indian grain mill laid in the Geiger woods. When the corps of army engineers, at the government's bidding, took over much of our land, Neil and Faye Geiger took the mill with them and later donated it to the town.

The last Civil War veteran in Markle was Billy Keller who lived on the corner of the county line and Morse Street.

When I was three years old my dad despaired of my life because I was "such a skinny little thing!" I heard him tell Mom,

"We're never going to raise her!" Then someone told them about a lady in Markle who could measure me for "short growth" and I would start growing! One time when we were at my grandparents Burley's house Aunt Nora told Mom, "You'd better try it because that kid looks awfully peaked!" So Mom and Aunt Nora loaded me into the buggy and drove to Markle where Mary Keller took me into her basement and measured me for "short growth"! Mom and Aunt Nora weren't allowed to watch as a woman could tell a man or man could tell a woman, but it was not a woman-to-woman thing!

She used a piece of string and measured me up and down and sideways, around my head and down my arms and legs. This string she gave to Mom with instructions to wind it around the single tree on the buggy and when it wore in two I was supposed to start growing. It worked after about twelve years, for then I became a dumpling and have remained so ever since! I always blamed Mary Keller. I think she used the wrong string because I was supposed to grow up—not out!

The Kellers happened to be great aunt and uncle to a dear boy whom I met and have loved for nearly fifty years. In 1942 we bought and lived in for ten years the house where I was measured for "short growth" when I was three.

Many businesses have come and gone from our town, but many still remain and the town has stretched out its arms and engulfed what was once the outskirts.

I am proud of my carpenter husband and sons and my brick mason son who have had a part in building our town. In this business one is privileged to get to know many people and some of them have become close friends.

We have enjoyed Travelogues this winter with Jo and Ted and have traveled many miles sitting on soft seats in the theater in Bluffton.

We were saddened this year on May 29th by the death of our dear friend Jim Dailey. He was only forty-five years old and a sudden heart attack took him from his wife and five young children!

Billy Kreisher died September 15th leaving a husband and two young sons. Dennis grew up with our kids and we mourn his loss. Billy was only thirty-seven years old.

The lake cottage is done and is a getaway place about every weekend.

Jim and Sandy planted a garden here and it is much nicer than mine. I guess the old dog will have to learn some new tricks.

Our dear family gathered once more to spend the night and early morning with us.

We are so thankful for this blessing.

1974

The boys were busy this year building a clinic for our doctors. Their continued faith in us makes us very humble and grateful. Our having built three of them each a new house and the mall is evidence of the excellence of workmanship, which Elmer is very proud of. Since he has retired I think he devotes more thought and energy to ongoing projects than before, if that is possible. A few people have asked him why he never has the name of his company on his truck as a way of advertising. His answer has always been, "If I do a good job, word will get around"—and I guess it has because he is always busy. Our sons are a great help and work well together. I know Elmer would have been greatly disappointed if they had not carried on in the line of work begun five or more generations ago. Grandpa Emerson used to tell the boys to learn a trade. He said, "You will never get rich, but you'll never starve to death either!"

Jeff and Byron help whenever they can but they are both interested in ball now. Jeff has a pet peeve and it is having to clean out the shop when the sawdust threatened to take over. He is very thorough in his work, and when he finished the job it is well done. Byron helps Kirby on the masonry end of the construction business.

Don is teaching his sons to work also. They have raised calves for 4-H and also for sale. Linda lined up the buckets in the kitchen and mixed the food after which the boys carried it to the barn. The barn was some distance from the house and each one carried two pails. I've always thought maybe Court might not now require extra-long sleeves if he had carried only one pail at a time! Since their farming days they, too, are learning the building trade. Once when they were visiting us for a few days they became interested in helping Grandpa in the shop. They were building ships and had more nails in them than wood. Whether to save nails or patience or both it's hard to say, but he told them they had enough boats and to go sail them somewhere. They said O.K. but just kept right on pounding. Elmer later told me that he said, "Didn't you boys hear what I said? You've got enough boats now!" Court's answer was, "We aren't building boats. We are building airplanes now."

We are proud of our son-in-law too. I have always been exceptionally proud of the beautiful bridge he designed and built across the Huron River in Ann Arbor. In my secret inner being it was my desire that he follow along in that line, but his desires led him in another direction. Now he is in building also. He and Elmer discuss for hours the pros and cons of whatever they discuss—Linda and I have our favorite things to talk about so we leave them to their pleasure and head for the kitchen or a shopping center! We like to go to flea markets, garden stores, dress shops, shoe stores, coffee shops, grocery stores, farm markets and just about anything that offers diversion from housekeeping. We think that what we do is much more interesting than what they do, but to each their own!

Our boys are doing a fine job on the clinic. It is next door to the mall and when the citizens of our town get put on a diet they can go right across the lawn and buy a candy bar!

Our doctors have made Markle their home and have become very much involved in our community. They are not only our doctors, they are also our friends. Once when Dr. Kinzer's house was under construction, Dawn and Mary were here with their children to discuss something with Elmer but visited with me also. Dawn said, "I want my house to look just like yours!" I was so surprised for I don't consider myself much of a housekeeper and thought she should aim higher than that! However, I don't think she was referring to the shabby furniture or the dust on the dining room table but to the aura of friendliness and welcome found here.

Elmer's parents were such friendly people. Everyone was welcome in their home but mine were stiff and formal when it came to fraternizing if they didn't know the people very well. In starting out my own marriage I tried to emulate the best of both families, and in case of a lack I made my own rules. One of the best qualities of my parents-in-law was their friendliness.

When we remodeled our house the front door opened to a small vestibule. Above the closet door at the end hangs a picture of Jesus knocking at the door. It is beautiful and as I look up I feel that looking upward is the position I should maintain for all of my life! Just as He would never turn anyone away, I feel that if I should, I might offend Him!

This spring the girls graciously offered to help me clean the cottage and get it ready for opening, and I welcomed the offer. It was also a time to get together and have a little fun. The way it turned out the "fun" was all at my expense! Jean, Shirley, Sandy and I headed north with all the cleaning equipment stowed in the trunk. Linda came from Jackson to meet us there.

Jean and I had been arguing about the name of the cottage next to ours and when we turned off the highway and entered on to the narrow road that led to our destination, I was more interested in proving my point than in watching the road. We slipped off the side and found ourselves mired in a seemingly bottomless marsh. Our feeble attempts to extricate the heavy car were not enough. Few people were at the lake, for it was early in the season, but one dear soul happened to be and he came to our rescue driving a little Volkswagen. He tried every which way but it was like a declawed house cat trying to motivate a lion! He offered to take me somewhere to get a wrecker and I was soon sailing toward a truck stop with S.O.S. written all over my face. Our neighbor had chores in another direction and left me to go back to the cottage in the wrecker. I looked askance at the thing and realized I couldn't reach the first step; the thing was so far off the ground! Before I had time to think about it very long, strong arms scooped me up and sat me on the seat, which was so high my feet didn't touch the floor! When we turned in at the cottage there were four grinning faces peering at me from the kitchen window, and when the driver deposited me on the ground those four were having convulsions! We were soon on solid ground, and after paying the driver I threatened the girls with expulsion from my will if they told Elmer. He thinks I operate with only half a brain anyway and this episode would go a long way toward proving him right!

By this time amid all the excitement we were ravenously hungry so we spent another considerable length of time quieting our nerves and our hunger! I don't remember how much cleaning we got done, but I'd say it was one of the least of our accomplishments!

True to their promises Elmer was unaware of our predicament—that is until about October. He and I went for a walk and stopped to talk to my benefactor who was winterizing his cottage, planning to spend part of the winter there. I said, "I don't think I'd like to be stuck up here in a bad snowstorm!" and he said, "I don't think that would be any different than being stuck in the mud!"—and thoroughly enjoyed himself at my expense. When we walked on Elmer said, "What was he talking about?"

Of course I had to confess and I don't know what he thought. I didn't ask him. He didn't say.

In this year all is well. Our grandchildren bring us much happiness and Christmas was a time of joy! The older ones never try to discourage the younger ones who still believe in Santa Claus, but often exchange knowing smirks with their peers.

Elmer follows doctor's orders much better than I ever could. My style of cooking has changed drastically, and it is a chore sometimes to figure out what to cook! Our pleasant trips to the Dutch Mill to have a delicious meal and more delicious thick malts have been curtailed, but he never complains. Farewell to 1974! Give us another good year in 1975 is my prayer!

1975

In this year of '75 I passed by my sixty-fifth birthday! As I sit down to evaluate the year I find my thoughts are more on evaluating my life.

I know I embarked on the right career, because it was the desire of my heart to have a home with someone I loved and to have real live babies to replace my dolls. I have never regretted my decision. In my career you get a taste of several careers. One doesn't go in depth in any one of them but gets a taste of many, and variety is the spice of life. I have nursed my children through colic, colds, mumps, measles, chicken pox, earaches, bloody noses, and all the little "ouchies" that childhood is victimized by. I have sewed little clothes for all of them, darned their little socks, patched their pants and sewed split seams. I have been a laundress, a housemaid, a baker, a cook and a disciplinarian. I have been a gardener and the head of a miniature-canning factory. I have been a teacher and when that didn't work, I preached! When that failed to bring results I rattled the cabinet drawer, which held the wood pancake turner! An application of that was long remembered!

In my early-married years I was a fashion designer and decorator. My children wore revamped clothing and our little girl was proud of her coats I fashioned from wool blankets. My sons wore shirts made from feed sacks. We didn't just go to the elevator and load on chicken feed but choose the ones with the most appropriate design to fit the need at the time. These sacks also were used for pillowcases, dishcloths, curtains, aprons, and many other articles.

Many crocheted rugs were made from worn out clothing. They were pretty on the floor and a comfort to bare feet.

In this reverie I ask myself what part of my life I enjoyed most. It is hard to say, for I have enjoyed every phase of it. However, I do hold dear the winter evenings when our children were small and they were still all ours. It was such a good feeling of accomplishment to know their tummies were full and that they were cozy and warm. Home was a haven where they felt safe and loved.

I guess my next love would have to be working in my flowerbeds. It is such a joy to walk around in early spring and see a new beginning in the brown earth. First to make an appearance is my one snowdrop. It has been in the same spot for years and I think of it as the herald of springtime. Next to bloom are the lovely crocus. They seem to defy the cold snaps and occasionally a snow. They show their sweetness as soon as the sun shines on them again. Then come the beautiful daffodils holding up their delicate cups to catch the sun or rain or to offer easy entrance to the pollen gathering bees. They seem to call forth the tulips, the creeping phlox, the bluebells and promises of roses evident in the fresh new growth beginning to show.

Later on, as I go about other chores that need my attention I look up and discover a miracle has happened! It seems that overnight the robins have settled their territorial disputes and are nesting in trees that have leafed out while I wasn't looking. Doves build such a shaky nest that I wonder how their young survive to be teenagers old enough to fly! Little Jenny Wren has occupied the same house for a long time and I always look forward to her coming each spring. Of course there are always the sparrows. For two years a pair of Flickers made a home in the old maple tree. They tore out a squirrel's nest and took over. I was glad for the change. Although the squirrels were a lot of fun to watch they can be destructive. For three years they had taken up residence in the old tree and we did enjoy watching the little ones perform their gymnastics among the branches. The day they decided to change residence was a day to behold! Being harassed by the flicker family and my one cat seemed to bring their activities to a sudden halt and they held a conference. The little ones had grown considerably but it was not hard to discern which was the mother. The six of them gathered around her as she chattered to them in squirrel language! I noticed one of them had a bare tail and later found the skin and hair in the flower bed so I knew that the antics of Tigger was the decisive factor in their decision to move!

When she started across the yard followed by the six I grabbed the binoculars and spent the morning watching them. When she rounded the house one decided he didn't want to go so ran up a tree in the back yard. There's one in every crowd, but she paid no attention to him. She crossed over Sharon and Bob's house, scampered over their front porch and behind the evergreens at the front of the house, never looking back to see if what's his name was coming or not. They arrived at the line fence where they held another conference, after which they were on their way again. I saw them turn and go up Bill and Marsha's lane, after that I lost them among Marsha's shrubs and flowers. For sometime Marsha had been telling me that they had wanted squirrels, but had trouble getting them to stay. Now she has seven! Later in the day I heard more chattering in the back yard and there was Mother giving her prodigal son what-for. She had trouble convincing him, but finally mother love won him over and they left, following the exact same course she had taken the first time!

We have little brown birds that nest low to the ground. They are tiny little things and when they forage for food they jump from one spot to another. I call them "Jumpers" because I don't know their real name. They get along well with the other birds, in fact all the birds get along well as long as each minds his own business. After territories are established they all settle down to the business of home construction. That being completed, the business of raising a family begins and they both work from dawn to dark at the job. While one searches for food the other stands guard at a distance and if trouble seems in the offing the guard goes through all kinds of didos to attract the attention of the marauder! They will also attack anything, regardless of size, that is a threat to their youngsters. I've seen my big cat tuck his tail and run for shelter when he got too nosy near a red bird's nest. The elusive little hummingbird piques my curiosity more than all the rest. How anything so small can possess so much energy is beyond me! Once when Elmer and I were enjoying an evening in our rocking chairs I heard a whirr and barely turning my head I glimpsed a hummer not six inches away which must have been attracted by the bright flowers in the mau-mau I was wearing! If a split second could be split into fifths, that's about how long it took him to change his course!

When the brown lawn of winter changes to green we are also blessed with golden flowers we neither plant nor tend. They are most generous in their distribution to rich and poor alike. I have written a little poem in their honor and to the sweetness of childhood, for what mother has never received at least one from her precious child!

Darling little grand child
With your gifts of gold
Overflowing chubby handsful
You don't know what you hold!

You praise your lovely mother
Many times a day
When you smilingly present to her
Your pretty, fresh bouquet!

She may receive an orchid
A rose corsage or two
But she'll not treasure one of them
Like these dandelions from you!

1976

This year there was a grandchild missing from the family gathering. Janelle spent Christmas with Murray and his parents at his grandmother's home in Florida. We missed her so much, but I guess we will have to get used to separations. Janelle got a diamond so that means the grandchildren are growing up and we will have to share them with the new world they will be entering!

Jerry and Jean won a trip to Bermuda this summer. I guess it is a beautiful place. When the cold winds of winter chill one to the bone I guess the islands call, but the heat of summer would be more than I could take.

We still had ten grandchildren at Christmas and they are all growing up so fast. Guess I didn't stop to realize that until one was missing at the table! We always put the younger ones together at one table, which means that Pat sits with Angie, Joni, Annette and Angenette. He came to me with sort of a long face and asked, "Grandma, why do I always have to sit with those girls?" He is a patient little guy and wouldn't have said anything if he had not been deeply disturbed, so next year Pat will have graduated to the upper class!

Pat is a quiet little fellow like Jeff but they are far apart in age, so he is always grouped with the younger children. Janelle was in the upper class with Mitch, Jeff, Byron, Court and Juli. When she arrived at the age between childhood and "young Lady Hood," she convinced her mother she was old enough for "heels." When the clan gathered at Grandpa's and Grandma's one Sunday, Janelle was a perfect lady for a while in her pretty new ruffled dress and shoes with little heels. In the afternoon we looked out and there she was playing baseball with the boys! Juli was contented in either group, but was really happiest when she could comb someone's hair! She loved long hair, which she didn't have. Her little auburn curls clung close to her little head and were beautiful, but not to a little girl who yearned for long hair!

Joni and Angie I call my "pin-up" girls. I have two pictures in my bedroom of a little blonde girl and one with raven locks. I call them Angie and Joni. They are old-fashioned pictures and some day I intend to present them to the two girls. They may not even want them but I have derived a lot of joy looking at them.

The twins hang together, and when Pat gets teased by one he has them both to contend with! They really like their cousin Pat.

It's so wonderful to reminisce over the years of their growing up—Mitchell and Janelle graduated this year, and I am a little stunned that the subjects they studied as history were current events when I was a senior! Time doesn't march on any more—it runs!

We had a wonderful trip to Williamsburg this summer with Harry and Marguerite. Elmer realized one of the dreams of his life: he got to go to Gettysburg. We had no use for a map of the place. He had it memorized and wherever he said to go to see something, we went and there it was! The stop-off at Gettysburg was the highlight of the whole trip for him. We enjoyed wonderful Williamsburg very much too.

It is always nice to come home after vacation, but this was a sad ending that greeted us when we reached Markle. There was a lot of activity at the Kinsey's and I knew immediately that Jean's mother had lost her battle with cancer. I felt so terrible that we weren't there with Jean and Jerry. I always love to share in my children's joys, and also to be with them in their sorrows!

Dorothy was a good person. I enjoyed knowing her and will miss her!

In this year of '76 we celebrated our nation's birthday!

Jean and I celebrated in a much different way. We headed up the Christmas program at church and celebrated when it was over. She did most of the legwork and I wrote, worried, wept, and waited for inspiration! Along with all else that Christmas entails around here, I doubted if I would ever see the other side of the mountain of accomplishment again—however, as always, persistence paid off and we came up with a pretty good program—or at least we thought so. The practices were terrible, but the program went off without a hitch and I sank back in my seat with relief and a thankful heart!

There was one part that I was especially fond of. I wanted somehow to combine Christmas with patriotism and came up with a parody to Abraham Lincoln's Gettysburg Address as follows—

Nineteen-hundred and seventy-six years ago, our Father, God, brought forth to this world His Son Jesus, conceived by Mary and dedicated to brotherly love forever and ever.

Now we are engaged in paying tribute to that Son, born to Mary so many years ago in a humble stable in Jerusalem.

We are met here to sing praises for His birth. We are met here to dedicate anew our lives in this struggle between right and wrong.

It is altogether fitting and proper that we should do this!

In this blessed land of freedom we can dedicate, we can consecrate, we can hallow our place in time! The Babe whose birth we celebrate has consecrated it, far beyond our power to add or detract.

The world will little note or long remember what we say here, but it can never forget what He did here.

It is for us, His people, to follow the precepts of this Holy Man who gave us the pattern for our lives. It is for us to remember our many blessings at this Christmas time, that from this great Savior we take increased devotion to that cause for which He gave the last full measure of devotion, that we here highly resolve that our Savior shall not have died in vain, that the world under God shall have a new revival of Christianity and that freedom to worship, dedication to duty and brotherly love shall not perish from the earth!

So ends another year with our blessed family minus one to share this beautiful season with us.

The New Year's party was celebrated at our house because on top of everything else I had fallen and was out of steam for several weeks. We dined on chicken soup with Carl and Mary, Garl and Mildred. Guy and Edna were in Florida soaking up the sunshine!

1977

can hardly believe this year has come and is almost gone already! It has been a busy one, that's for sure! We had a real snowstorm in January. You would think that boredom would set in cooped up as we were but we were kept busy running from window to window to watch!

The day of Carl and Mary's 50th wedding anniversary was a bad, icy day, and I was scared silly about driving. After two or three telephone calls Mary said someone would come for us. While I was protesting Dick and Louella came whizzing in the driveway and away we went! We went to church with their whole family. It was a pleasure because many of our old friends were at Boehmer and many we hadn't seen for a long time. We went to Carl's for lunch and afterward to the Sportsmen's Club for the reception. What a nice day! What wonderful friends! We have shared so many experiences. In these more affluent times we marvel at the fact that we made it through the Depression. We were well equipped and none of us suffered from it because we had always been poor as church-mice and you just don't miss something you never had! Work was scarce but we were not paying $400 a month rent either! In the afternoon Jean and Jerry came and all too soon the day was at an end and we came sliding safely home.

Don and Linda bought a home on Clark Lake. It is a far cry from what they were used to, but Don is already planning on changes to be made.

Another "first" happened on July 8th. Our first granddaughter was married! It was a beautiful wedding but the weather was extremely hot as the wedding anniversary was extremely cold!

Just six days after she was married, Jerry had a bad accident. The boys were putting a cover on the vault at the bank. It was of poured concrete and in such cramped quarters that they had to crawl around to accomplish what they had to do. Jerry burned both legs badly. Larry wore heavier pants and was spared from the severe burns that Jerry suffered. When Janelle came home after the wedding trip she could hardly believe what had happened to her dad! She and Murray are getting ready to move into their apartment.

The bank job is done and I so often think about the spot in our fair town where the bank is situated. An asphalt parking lot covers the spot where once stood a sweet little house, surrounded by an iron fence. There were flowers and vines around the house and a little garden on the back of the lot. At night a faint little ray of light behind a lace curtain failed to penetrate far into the darkness. Trees along the sidewalk cast long shadows from the small streetlight. Unless there was a full moon, the corner was somewhat dark which added a measure of mystery as to what went on there. Girls in two and threes passed by giggling and having a great time.

As soon as my mother would allow me to cross Morse Street without her (at around age thirteen) my girlfriend and I joined the promenade. Would you believe it? There were *boys* standing on the corner in front of the little house! They teased the girls and chased them laughing on their way. My friend Helen and I walked past pretending not to notice them. They didn't notice us either! I never could figure out whether it was my red hair or my pigeon-toed shuffle that was a detriment to us!

Around the fourth of July, that corner was pure bedlam—boys throwing firecrackers at girls' feet and girls jumping and screaming and running across the street where they walked the length of the block and came right back for more!

My friend Helen and I soon learned the meaning of the word "popular." It was an adjective that didn't apply to us! We never got blown into a state of hysteria, not even with a firecracker for the two of us. We soon became contented to chew on our gumdrops and watch from the sidelines.

I wonder if our good bank president, Don, and his capable workers realize that romances blossomed and life commitments may have been made under the tree that once graced the street in front of their establishment.

Of all the boys who stood on the corner or the girls who walked past, I wonder how many have ever appreciated the patience of the little lady behind the oil lamp, behind the lace curtain, behind the window of the little house behind the iron fence!

The family spent Thanksgiving with Jim and Sandy. We always have such good times when we get together. My birthday was celebrated with all the family being together at Kirby and Shirley's. Their home is so nice with a big yard for all the kids to play in. They have a big garden too and raise a lot of good things to eat and can for winter. All of our girls make us very proud. They are all good managers of their time and finances, and a blessing to their husbands.

We will soon be having new neighbors as we sold an acre on the north side to Phil and Sharon Hosier. They will soon be starting a new house.

Elmer is not a bit well and gets tired so easily. I worry about him and try to spare him whatever I think might upset him. In October when Jerry came in from the shop with his finger all chewed up, I managed to attend to him, get him in the car with his arm sticking up in the air and take him to the emergency room. Elmer had been resting in his den and didn't know about it until Jerry was on the way to the hospital in Fort Wayne. I felt just as bad as I did when Jerry got hurt as a little boy. He has been pretty lucky until this year. Kirby fell off his bike and cracked his shoulder blade once when he and Linda were racing to the post office to get Mrs. Elick's paper for her, and was so uncomfortable in his bandages. The poor little fellow had trouble resting and I held him for several nights so he could sleep. Jim getting shot was the worst disaster of all! I guess boys are more accident prone than girls—because Linda, except for the little "ouchies" that accompany childhood, was pretty lucky. She did drop a cup on her toe one time and cried most of the night. All the hours spent rocking and consoling were well worth it, because I am mighty proud of the brood we raised! Elmer was all thumbs when it came to the nursing department, but that was all right. He worked hard and provided us with a good home. His responsibilities were great and I wouldn't have traded jobs with him. He often said how much he appreciated what I did and that he could never do it. I guess we were a pretty good team. At least we weren't jockeying for each other's jobs!

Beautiful October flew past so quickly I hardly had time to enjoy it. Elmer went to the hospital for surgery and was much slower recovering than the first time. I wish it were possible to take all the pain myself—it is so dreadful to see those you love cope with it! He is so thin and haggard looking. I long to bake him a big cake, or bring him a tall glass of malted milk that he used to love so much, but all these good things are a no-no for him!

Christmas has come and gone. All the families were home and we enjoyed them as usual.

New Year's was spent with Carl and Mary. Garl and Mildred babysat. Guy and Edna were in Florida.

I find myself clinging to the old year because I am fearful of what the new year has in store for us!

1978

It is time to say goodbye to 1978. It was been a good year. We are all well and able to enjoy life, which is a great thing to be thankful for. The biggest thing was the great snow! It came January 25th and was still on the ground back of the garage on the 13th of April! On the 5th of February we escaped and went on a much looked-forward-to cruise. We were thankful for Jerry and Jean who kept an eye on us when they could find us. We had a glorious time. Took our fist plane ride and first ship ride. We got better acquainted with our neighbors, and got to spend time with Harry and Marguerite. Berthel and Marshall were in the cabin on one side of us and Jerry and Jean on the other. We had a wonderful time and will never cease to be thankful to Jean who kept pestering us 'til we consented to go! There were ten couples plus Wilda. Harry and Marguerite, Clair and Palace Weibke, Marshall and Berthel Lowery, Rex and Marilyn Douglass, Pat and Peg Roebuck, Ernie and Martha Thoma, Barb and Hube Girvin, Ed and Rheda Espich, Jerry and Jean and, of course, us.

This year marks a new beginning for Jeff, Court and Byron. They graduated from high school in the spring and are all three off to college. Jeff is at IU, Court at JC in Jackson and Byron at Indiana State. Murray is in his third year at Huntington and Mitchell just finished a year-and-a-half at JC and has now enrolled in Ypsilanti.

Janelle celebrated one year of marriage in July and is very happy. We hope all the others will be able to find happiness with as good of a partner as Janelle has found in Murray.

Juli is still working on her music and does very well with it. She is active in church and school, and I know both places are better for having our Juli there.

Angela will be twelve in a few days and I know her daddy and mother can hardly believe it either. She loves baseball, basketball and skateboarding.

Joni will soon have a birthday too. Maybe this year we will get to spend it with her. For two years now we have been gone and we missed being with her. Joni loves piano and does very well. She also likes and plays baseball. So far, she and Angie have been on opposite teams. I wish they could play together like Byron and Jeff did and had so much fun.

The twins haven't started a career yet. They are busy little girls and are doing well in school. They are growing up much too fast, because they are our babies.

How could I have forgotten Pat?—My old checker-playing partner—forgive me, Pat! Pat is too young for girls, too old for toys so he just has fun with his dog. He likes his new school, and will soon be the only one left at home when Court goes away to college.

I have been busy since March knitting and crocheting. Made six afghans and a rug for grandchildren. Still have four more to go—no, five, because in a weak moment I promised one to the firemen to raise money for "Wildcat" days. They are a deserving group, so I intend to make my promise good. Bruce and Erma surprised us with a visit. We enjoy them so much and wish they hadn't gone to Florida to live. We enjoyed our last class reunion at Harry and Marguerites. They are going to move back to town. It is time the rest of us take our turn anyway. The '79 reunion will be with Esther Moore.

About a week ago the switch on our car went bad and Marv Highlen installed a new one. I immediately set about replacing the old key with the new one and thought I might as well replace the one on the extra set, which is seldom used. I was very careful to get them just right on both sets. I threw the old keys in the garbage can, because this household has more keys that nobody knows where they belong than any place in town. My husband is a saver and when he starts to hunt for something, it is easier to go buy another and less time consuming than rummaging through all his treasured possessions.

The only things in my department that I can't find are the things that I put in a special place so I will know right where they are.

On this very special morning of September 20th, I awoke remembering it was our wedding anniversary. I always like to lie and listen to the morning. The martins are gone now, but there are other sounds equally beautiful. I could also hear my husband and sons talking over the affairs of the day. Then I heard a loud "SHE..." in a nasty tone of voice. When he calls me "she," instead of using my name or saying "your mother," I *know* there's stormy weather ahead. I should have just stayed in bed all day, but I grabbed my robe and hurried out to ascertain the cause of his tone of voice.

"You threw away the keys to my Sprint." (He's always accusing me of things I'm guilty of.)

"I did not—" etc., etc. The next twenty minutes were spent frantically fitting keys into keyholes and searching for the missing set. He finally found a set with "Olds 80" written right on the tag. His evidence was indisputable—there he had me, cold turkey. My first irrational impulse was to chase the garbage truck, but he had gone the day before unmindful of the precious cargo he carried. I next rushed into the living room to try to ease my frustration by beating the pants off of "Old Sol." After losing three games, I discovered I was playing with only fifty-one cards. I guess that's about par for the course for someone who, for some time, has been rowing her boat with one oar out of the water.

In the afternoon I looked out there, and there was Marv again. This time with a new switch for the truck. I'll bet he wonders what goes on around here. He is not alone. Sometimes I wonder too.

My keys now hang on one side of the wall and the truck keys on the other, and I hope that "Ne'er the twaine shall meet." Neither of us wished the other a "Happy Anniversary," because it just was not the kind of a day that you wanted to *"reach out and touch someone."*

My husband can be thankful that his is a monogamous marriage—what if he were in King Solomon's shoes?

We had a nice Thanksgiving at Jim and Sandy's house. The whole family was there except Mitchie who flew to Arkansas to visit a school buddy who is in the service there. Sandy's parents were with us too. Jim and Sandy's home is so nice and roomy and I'm glad the leftover turkey is there instead of here. Maybe I'll learn to like turkey again!

We had a nice New Year's party with Garl and Mildred, Carl and Mary. Carl and Mary were hosts and took us to a Japanese restaurant in Fort Wayne where the chef cooked our meal in front of us. We even tried eating with chopsticks! Because of the fog we spent the evening at our house where we just sat around and talked. We love to reminisce and with all three couples we failed to get the past straightened out to our satisfaction!

We haven't gone very many places this summer. Just enjoyed being home. Went to an IU football game but went more to see Jeff than to see the game. Went with Shirley once to take Byron back to school. We are still going to travelogues and enjoying them. Had a nice garden this year and have lots of good fruit and vegetables in the freezer. Hope for strength and health to do the same this year. It won't be a very happy time when I have to give up my garden! The snow is coming down softly today and it is very peaceful and beautiful. I don't see any activity around the bird feeder, so they must all be holed in for the winter too.

1979 is a blank page as yet. Each year I wonder what I will write next year. Always ask for good health for our family. This year I ask for protection and love for little Jeremy. May his time with Kirby and Shirley be something he will never forget, and may it inspire him to live a good life and make something good of himself. May his mother find a new way of life and come to realize there's only one way to live—the right way.

God be with us all in '79.

Uncle Jesse died in September.

Ward Bailey died.

1979

can't seem to convince myself that we have come to within a year of being married fifty years! Where did the time go?

As I look back there isn't much that I would change. Small successes have brought happiness and reverses have made me strong. I have been blessed with a good husband and good healthy children who lead good lives and put forth their best efforts to raise their children to be responsible citizens. There is one wish that is uppermost in my mind at this time and that is that my husband's health might improve. He has had to substitute good food with watery milk, Egg Beaters, Fleischmann's margarine, etc. Oh! How we miss warm summer evening trips to the Dutch Mill in Bluffton for a tenderloin sandwich and a vanilla malt!

I just solved this cryptogram in my crossword puzzle book and think it is a gem: "It may be bad manners to talk with your mouth full, but it isn't too good, either, if you speak when your head is empty."

I wouldn't be surprised if it doesn't also apply to writing, but a mini-catastrophe at our house about 7:00 this morning prompts me to give some advice of my own: "*Always* screw the lid on tight." I arose on this beautiful, cool morning confident I was going to have a nice day. This was the day I would make raspberry jelly. I had hoarded this juice for some time waiting for a cool day. It takes lots of berries to make a quart of juice—also a good measure of endurance of briar scratches, mosquito bites, poison ivy, and a relentless sun beating down on one's head. I tested to make sure the juice was still good, placed the lid on loosely and set it back in the refrigerator until I had my coffee.

When my "soulmate" reached for the milk, he had to move the juice lifting it by the lid. I heard a thud and when I turned around it looked like someone had murdered Dracula right in front of the refrigerator, under it and in it.

We exchanged some casual remarks, "which is the understatement of the year," as I started to mop—a foolish thing to do but a mop in hand was better than a rolling pin just then. He soon disappeared out of doors and when I stood up, I had purple knees and a purple tail on my robe and nightgown. I grabbed a bucket and ran hot water over the stains as I stood there with my glasses on. I didn't care if he came in or not. He deserved to see the ugly side of life. Someday I may laugh—but not today, not tomorrow—maybe Sunday.

Bless Alan Brown from Warren. At this very moment he has all his equipment out there trying to restore the carpet to normal.

We had a nice garden this year and have a lot of goodies in cans and in our freezer. Old habits die hard and we have processed about the same amount as when four hungry kids surrounded our table three times a day! Guess it's time to cut back! Our flowers outdid themselves this year and we enjoyed their beauty longer than usual because of the late frost.

Where else in the world could a person live and be privileged to enjoy the changing of the seasons as we lucky Hoosiers do? If you don't like the weather today, just hang in there because it will be different tomorrow! If the heat of summer is getting you down just be patient because before you know it autumn has come and gone and you can open your door and be cool! If you grow tired of being cozy eating popcorn in front of the TV, don't despair, for some morning you will spy a robin on the lawn and spring will have arrived! Where else but in Indiana? We have been able to do a little traveling but are always glad to get home. We will never get a speeding ticket leaving home, but the nearer we get on our return, the faster we go!

I am looking forward to next year and wonder what it will be like being married for fifty years! I guess it won't be much different than being married for forty-nine! Will tell you all about it next year!

1980

The snow is coming down gently today and hardly a leftover leaf is moving as I sit me down to record the events of the wonderful year just past! In June we helped Dorothy and Darwin celebrate their anniversary. That was the last time I ever saw Darwin's sisters and brothers, but we had a good time that day! With Mary and Raymond in Tennessee and Dorothy and Darwin in Ohio, it is a rare occasion when we can all be together and we make the most of it when we can.

Our garden shows signs of neglect, for we have so many things to think about and weeds are not one of them! I went with Shirley to Marion one day and was lucky enough to find a dress for our anniversary and she found a beautiful dress for Byron and Cindy's wedding! It seems like I have spent the whole year in preparation! One of the hardest tasks I had was getting my husband to go shopping—he doesn't need a new suit because the old one isn't worn out yet, and he definitely doesn't need a new pair of shoes, because "See here, the soles are still good!" I passed a milestone when that chore was accomplished!

We invited our family to a "Thank You!" party at the Gateway Inn on September 19th because we knew they had gone to a lot of trouble and expense for us. It was so wonderful to have our beloved family at one big, long table! You realize that after graduations and weddings these joys are bound to be limited! However, the college kids and the wedded kids all made it!

I have no idea how many chickens laid down their lives that night to appease the hunger of all who gathered there, but it was no small amount! Kyle Legg outdid himself. The food was so delicious! After the meal a big package was presented to us. We were overjoyed to receive a beautiful picture of our family taken in our beautiful park. Then a smaller gift made its appearance and it was a lovely gold locket set from my husband! My dear granddaughters were all around me and fastened it for me because I was so overcome with surprise that my nervous hands refused to function!

Next morning we all gathered together at church and all sat in pews marked especially for us! Rev. Lloyd Hall introduced us all (as if we hadn't lived here for years) and after a hearty applause he said, "Elmer, does it seem like fifty years since you have been married?"— and my loving husband answered, "Fifty l-o-n-g, l-o-n-g years!"

After a hurried lunch we got ready to go back to the church for a happy reunion with friends. I sort of have a reputation for being a worrywart and the thought hit me "What if nobody comes!"

I needn't have worried. I think everybody we ever knew was there and we had a wonderful time. Our girls left nothing to be desired in way of decorations. The three-tiered cake and all the sheet cakes disappeared like magic. So did the dishes of nuts and mints and punch. We ran out of all we thought we'd need and all the extras on hand in case it was needed. Some kind soul opened the grocery store so the punch bowl could be replenished. I think the caterer must have been about out of her mind when the day finally came to an end and she could pack up all her empty dishes, cups, jugs and boxes and limp back to Bluffton!

It was so great to see so many people who mean so much to both of us, new friends, old friends, cousins, brothers and sisters, nephews and nieces and our own dear children and grandchildren! Did I miss anybody?

Many pictures were taken and I know they will always be treasured!

Added to all the joy in our hearts was the beautiful day that Mother Nature bestowed on us. Many times September is cold or rainy or both, but the sky was a beautiful picture with snowy clouds sailing high in the blue!

When we said goodbye to the last guest we were chased out by our children because we were both about ready to drop! I know Elmer was tired. I had "tennis elbow" all the way to my shoulders and my feet were overflowing my new shoes! When we got home he marched straight for the bedroom, and after I sprinkled a little water on the boutonniere and corsage, I followed suit. I drew the drapes to shut out the sun, and then I was off to dreamland too!

Such lovely memories to carry into our tomorrows!

Christmas has come and gone and left us with a lovely new member in our family. Byron and Cindy were married December 20th in a beautiful ceremony in her church. Now we have two grandchildren married and should be feeling somewhat old, but it seems that life gets more interesting every day! I'm tired now, but I know that when spring comes again, I will be rested and ready to welcome the flowers that are also resting!

History & Prose

A Very Brief History of the Mossburg Family

*R*ev. Henry Mossburg was born in Germany in 1776 and brought to this country at the age of six months. He is reputed to have had five brothers but we have no confirmation of this. We do know that he was the only one to move to this state. His parents settled in Maryland and began clearing land for farming.

Henry, at an early age, left home and went to Virginia in search of work. Very little is known of his early life, except that he became a Christian church minister and met the Thrailkill family. Around 1804 he married Jane Thrailkill and moved to Clinton County, Ohio. Mrs. Mossburg was a native of Virginia and of French ancestry. While serving with the Army during the war of 1812, he contracted consumption and remained in poor health the remainder of his life. To this union was born nine children, but we do not have the names of them all.

In 1827 the family moved to Delaware County, Indiana, where they had purchased twenty acres of land which he soon sold and entered eighty acres from the government. This he partially improved and then sold it in 1837 and moved to Liberty Township, Wells County, where the Mossburg Cemetery is now located. His was the second family to locate in Liberty Township.

In the fall of 1838, while walking near the cabin, he set a stick in the ground and told a son that he was to be buried there. Knowing the time of death was close, a son Daniel set out for Muncie, the nearest market, to purchase his burial clothes. He was nineteen years old at this time and returned just as his father passed away. A neighbor had brought some poplar with him to build a wagon box, but he donated this for a coffin and with eight-penny nails the coffin was built and the father was buried on the previous selected spot November 2, 1838. This was the first white man buried in Liberty Township and fence rails were laid over the grave to keep wolves from digging up the remains. Mrs. Mossburg lived in the cabin until 1845 when another son Henry was married and she went to live with him until she passed away in 1872. She is buried beside her husband in the Mossburg Cemetery.

Our subject now becomes the second son and fifth child of Rev. Henry and Jane (Thrailkill) Mossburg, born in Clinton County, Ohio, March 16, 1819. As previously mentioned, he was nineteen years old when his father passed away in Liberty Township, Wells County, November 2, 1838. In 1840 he met Elizabeth Brown, daughter of Elisha Brown, at an Indian dance on the south bank of the Wabash River and the west side of the north end south road near the point where the Rockcreek and Wabash rivers meet.

An intimacy sprang up between them and they were married January 6, 1842. At this time Daniel was trapping and catching coons and other fur-bearing pelts. He sold the pelts for $50 and entered forty acres in Salamonie Township, Huntington County. Here he and his wife built a cabin and here they resided until death. This acreage lies 1/2 mile north and 1/2 mile west of Buckeye Station. Daniel, aside from tending his forty acres, was a furniture and coffin builder. During this time he had the most complete cabinet shop in Huntington County.

The wife, Elizabeth Brown, was born in Wilkes County, North Carolina, on July 11, 1817, and came to Delaware County, Indiana, at an early age. In 1838 she came with her parents to Wells County. Daniel passed away March 21, 1900 and Elizabeth four days later. They are both buried in the Mossburg Cemetery. To their union was born eight children, five living to maturity.

Starting the next generation we find Daniel P. Mossburg, son of Daniel and Elizabeth Mossburg, fifth child of eight children. He was born April 23, 1852, in the cabin of his grandfather. His complete life was spent in Salamonie Township, Huntington County, Indiana. He became a lover of woodwork but unlike his father, he became a hewer and builder of barns.

Very little is know about the wife of Daniel P. except that her name was Catherine Shoemaker, daughter of Archibold and Sarah Shoemaker, and she was born July 25, 1855. The couple was married at the bride's home June 5, 1872, by Rev. Samuel Swaim. At the time of their marriage they purchased eighty acres of land two miles east and one-half mile north of Warren, Indiana, or one mile west of Buckeye Station. To this union was born eight boys and three girls. We do not know how long they resided on the farm but it was sometime after the death of Catherine which occurred November 28, 1899.

After the farm was sold Daniel P. remarried and moved to Warren. By this time most of the children had left home and started on their own. The only things we know about this second marriage was that her name was Clara, and it only lasted a short time.

This was the time that Warren was a rip-roaring oil town and they were having trouble keeping a marshal. Daniel P. made the statement around town that if given the chance he would straighten it up. So when the last marshal resigned, the town council appointed Daniel P. to the job. Being a man who was reputed at not being afraid of the devil he took to the street and saloons and starting swinging his nightstick. This won him the applause of the town and for his dedication to duty, he remained marshal for the next twenty years. By this time he was getting quite elderly, so he sold his few possessions and lived with his children until March 5, 1937. He passed away at the age of eighty-five years. He and his wife are buried in the Mossburg Cemetery.

The next generation starts with the first child of Daniel P. and Catherine (Shoemaker) Mossburg, Emerson F. Mossburg. He was born August 7, 1873, in Salamonie Township, Huntington County, Indiana. Following in the footsteps of the previous two generations, his entire life was spent in Huntington and Wells county area. During his growing up years he hired out to different farmers of the area but after marriage he became a house and barn builder.

Hannah Aby Irwin was born November 3, 1876, in a log cabin 4 miles east of Warren, Indiana, or a half-mile south and one mile east of Buckeye Station, just inside the Huntington-Wells county line. She always answered to the name of Aby. She and Emerson F. were acquaintances from childhood, each going to the same school, what little they went, and at times worked for the same farmers, she as a housemaid and he as a farmhand. She was the eighth child of twelve born to John Lorenze and Mary Ann (Edgar) Irwin.

Emerson F. and Hannah Aby were united in marriage October 6, 1900, at the groom's home by Rev. Samuel Swaim. They set up housekeeping just a quarter-mile south of the birthplace of the groom. To the union was born four children. Edith was born on October 28, 1901 and passed away February 20, 1920, from the flu epidemic that was running rampant that winter. Howard was born on October 23, 1904, Elmer on September 23, 1906, and Grace on February 18, 1911. Howard passed away October 29, 1974. The other two are still living.

They purchased their first home in 1904, a two-bedroom house, a barn and three acres of land, two miles west of Liberty Center. In 1921 this was sold and they purchased ten acres one-and-a-quarter miles north of Mount Zion. Here they lived until Mrs. Mossburg passed away on January 17, 1941. The place was then sold and Mr. Mossburg moved to Markle in small quarters where Elmer was living. In his last years, he divided his time by staying with Elmer and Grace. On February 15, 1953, he passed away at the home of Elmer and was buried in the Mossburg Cemetery beside his wife.

We now pick up the life of Elmer Mossburg, the third child of Emerson F. and Hannah Aby (Irwin) Mossburg. As was previously stated he was born on September 23, 1906, and like the previous three generations has spent his entire life within ten miles of where he was born. He was born two miles west of Liberty Center and attended a little country school through his first eight grades. He then attended four years of high school at Liberty Center and received his diploma April 20, 1924. During his high school years and two years after graduation he hired out to farmers, then started working with his father in the building trade, which he pursued the rest of his working years.

Hilda Alfreda Dennis was born in Union Township, Huntingdon County, Indiana, July 27, 1910 to Alfred Frances Dennis and Margaret May (Burley) Dennis. She was the oldest of four daughters born to this union. Her parents descended from John C. Dennis and Clara Virginia (Denny) Dennis on the father's side and John Wallace Burley and Mary Magdeline (Lahr) Burley on her mother's side. Both families were generally considered as residents of Union Township Huntington and Union Township Wells County. Her father was a handyman and worked for several employers at several trades until middle-age when he purchased a farm and became his own employer.

Alfreda, the name she answered to, attended several schools and on April 22, 1929, graduated from high school at Lafayette Central, Allen County, Indiana. She worked as a housemaid and two partial years as a G.E. employee before becoming a housewife.

Elmer and Alfreda's first meeting was at a school class party in the early spring of 1927. They did not, however, become attracted to each other until the late spring of 1928. The seeds of admiration and respect took root and began growing. On September 20, 1930, they were pronounced man and wife by Rev. I.R. Beery the Brethren Church Minister in Markle.

They rented a house two miles west of Liberty Center and one-and-a-half miles south for five dollars a month. Times were really rough for there was very little money and little work. But if you had no obligations and no debts you could get by. Many are the books that are written about these times so we will not dwell on them.

To this union was born four children, Jerry A., April 14, 1934, Linda G., February 14, 1938, Kirby D., September 22, 1940, and James H., December 7, 1946.

Elmer and Alfreda purchased their first home in Buckeye Station in the spring of 1932 for $450. Money was so scarce that it took over four years to pay this debt. Their first three children were born here, but James didn't make an appearance until they had moved to Markle. In 1936 times began to improve and in the fall of 1938 Elmer took his gang and started working in Fort Wayne almost entirely, building houses on the FHA plan. Since moving to Markle would put them much closer to their work, they rented their house in Buckeye and moved to a rental in Markle. This worked much better until the beginning of World War II, for this closed down all their operations in Fort Wayne. In the spring of 1942 they sold their home in Buckeye and purchased a home in Markle.

They lived inside the city limits of Markle until 1952 when they sold their home and purchased a house and ten acres just a short distance north of Markle on State Road #3 and still live there. Jerry, their eldest son, graduated from Markle High School and after a hitch in the army, formed a partnership with his father and started the fifth generation of woodworkers. They also expanded into light industrial construction. Jim, the youngest, graduated from Lancaster Central in 1965, served his hitch in Vietnam and on his return joined his father's construction gang.

In 1971, the father turned the business over to Jerry and Jim; they formed a partnership and the father retired. Of the four children, they are all married and have families. Jerry married Norma Jean Kinsey and they have two children, Janelle and Jeffery. Linda Gay married Donavon Carl and they have three boys, Mitchell, Courtney and Patrick. Kirby married Shirley Mae Merchant and they have three children, Byron, Juli and Joni. Kirby continued in the building trade but as a masonry contractor. Jim married Sandra Hahn and they have three children, Angela, Angenette and Annette who are twins. This is the way it is March 6, 1982.

Written by Elmer Mossburg

Over to Aunt Lou's

In our part of the country people say, "Come up," or, "Come down" or "Come over to see us sometime." We went "to" town, we went "down" to Grandpa Burley's house, "up" to see Grandpa and Grandma Dennis, but we went "over" to Aunt Lou's house!

My sister and I looked forward to a visit to her house from the moment we heard our mother tell our father, "I guess I'll go over to Aunt Lou's next week."

We were fed our supper and "bedded down" early on the night preceding "A.L. Day" and routed out next morning before daybreak to start the six-mile journey.

Dad always gave a lot of last-minute instructions like, "Now don't stay 'til plum dark and don't run that horse to death, neither! When she starts to lather, slow down!" He needn't have worried because Mom sat there stiff as a poker, torso bent forward, arms straight out in front of her, holding on to the lines for dear life! I used to think that if her arms were a little longer she wouldn't need any lines at all, but could grab a bit on each side and steer from where she sat. Mama was always afraid the horse would get scared and run away. I don't think Nellie was half as scared as Mama was. As soon as she heard the word "whoa," she hunkered her head down between her shoulders and was fast asleep before the buggy wheels stopped turning. The only way we could tell she was alive was that she switched her tail when a fly chewed to deeply for comfort. We weren't really sure then because people used to say that snakes didn't die until after sundown and their tails stopped wriggling no matter what time they were killed. Maybe since Mama was never allowed to stay anywhere "'til dark," old Nellie just never got a chance to die completely.

Aunt Lou was what was known as "well fixed." That meant she had plenty of this world's goods and there was plenty of Aunt Lou! She never saw bathroom scales but I know she would have had to stand twice to weigh herself. She was a German woman good as anyone God put breath in. Her speech was a strange mixture of German and English, which we kids could only half-understand. We did understand, however, the huge wedges of pie she fed us. The nearer old Nellie carried us to her door the harder my gastric juices worked and when we got just inside the kitchen I'd be all knotted up inside with hunger. The more Mama tried to "shush" me, the hungrier I became and could no longer hold back my tears. Inevitably a great round cookie was forced upon me for Aunt Lou was of the opinion that food would cure anything, and it did cure what was wrong with me! My sister never said a word but sat crumpling the hem of her dress with nervous little fingers 'til she got a cookie too. The sneaky little thing got hers for free and I had to work for mine! I'd hurry and eat mine then coax her out of earshot of Mama and Aunt Lou to wheedle her out of half of hers. If she refused to cooperate I just downed her and took it away from her, which, of course, sent her to Mama bawling incriminations against me. The upshot of it was that the "good child" got another cookie while I inhaled the cookie dust, which was all that was left after I had wrestled it away from her.

Aunt Lou's dinner table was a thing of beauty. Our meals today are built around one meat, two or three vegetables and a dessert. At Aunt Lou's house there was served three or four kinds of meat, half-a-dozen vegetables, and four or five desserts, all at one meal. You ate until you could swallow no more so you just sat and chewed and chewed on the last bite.

Aunt Lou made her own butter, cottage cheese, pickles, preserves, jellies, kraut, bread and everything that went into our mouths. They butchered hogs, calves, sheep and chickens. The meat was sugar-cured or fried down. They raised cane, which was made into sorghum, and kept bees, which produced honey. It was kept in five-gallon jars and when she would lift the lid I'd nearly pass out from the delicate, palatable aroma. They had maple trees and consequently, maple molasses. I never saw so much of everything and nothing was allowed to go to waste although a lot of it went to waist on Aunt Lou. It's no wonder her figure knew no bounds.

After a bounteous meal was over the perishables were put down in the cold, black cellar, but what remained was left on the table and covered over with a long cloth. About an hour after the meal was over we were hungry again so we were allowed to lift the big circus tent with its spoon-holder center pole to choose whatever appealed to us.

When we started for home, Aunt Lou scooped up everything that could travel and we ate all the way home. By suppertime I could not eat another bite, and Dad would say, "what's the matter with this kid, she isn't eatin?" Then he would put his rough hand on my forehead to see if I was feverish. Just the thought of food made me break out in a cold sweat and he was sure Mama had run us in to something traipsing all over the country!

Aunt Lou's house was called a square-type house. It was two stories high with the parlor and dining room on one side of an entrance hall. On the other side was the bedroom and a kitchen, dining and a sitting room. The bedroom is indistinct in my memory but I do remember the big bed with its billowy feather ticks. I never knew Uncle John, who died before I was born, nor did I ever know what took him from this world, but now when I recall the billowy feather bed, billowy Aunt Lou, and the billowy feather-tick she used as a cover, I think he may have died in self-defense.

We played in the kitchen side of the house and considered the huge hallway sort of a no-man's-land beyond which lay wonderland, the parlor. I remember what a treat it was just to look through the doorway. We stood there with chills running up and down our sides for the room had a mysterious, chilling fascination for us and we would never venture beyond the doorway without Mama or Aunt Lou. It was never used that I know of, unless perhaps Aunt Lou's foster daughter sat in there when her beau came calling. The room was so dark and foreboding with the shades always drawn to the sill that it would have taken someone far braver than I to have sat in there at night without Mama. I don't know what kept moths from devouring the Brussels carpet inch-by-inch unless moths are just one of our modern inconveniences.

Fine lace curtains hung at the windows, fell to the floor and spread out fan-shaped over the carpet. You just weren't anybody if your curtains didn't lie on the floor thus and so. I don't recall seeing curtains anywhere else in the house but in the parlor. We had to be very careful where we put our feet.

In the center of the room stood a beautiful table with carved legs. On it and in the same spot for years was an album with a green velvet cover, a beautiful lamp with roses on the bowl and shade, and a big seashell that we were allowed to put our ear against to listen to the sound of the sea. I don't know what adventurous scamp in our family had ever been far enough away from Indiana to have acquired a seashell, but there it lay, in all its glory, boasting of far-away places.

In the corner stood the organ which was supposed to be a thing of beauty. It had miniature newel posts and numerous shelves to hold bric-a-brac. In the top was a mirror so small you scanned your face a pore at a time. All the little shelves were so laden with so many things that if one laid his toothpick down to keep from inhaling it when he sang he might as well consider it one with the curios because he could never find it again!

Many people cherish these old monstrosities but I wouldn't give one of the things houseroom. I always associate them with tall, narrow windows, and slippery horsehair sofas, which I hate.

In Aunt Lou's parlor was a black horsehair sofa. I'd defy any body to make love to a girl seated on one of these things. It must have been quite disconcerting after having summed up the courage to pop the question to let loose of the sofa arm long enough to hold her hand and find one self sitting on the floor. No wonder so many betrothals were agreed upon in the buggy on the way home. A man could wind the lines around the buggy whip and trust his horse but he couldn't trust a horsehair sofa.

After these visits to Aunt Lou's house and the conducted tour through her parlor our own home always looked bare and dull. Still there was no room in our house where I felt afraid or ill at ease. I sincerely hope the "family" room in our modern homes does not eventually elevate the living room to the same high plane the parlor occupied in the homes of yesterday. I can't believe I could get so close to people where I had to herd them through the front door to a seldom-used room where I had to raise the shades and straighten the tie on my great-great-grandfather's picture before I could start a conversation.

The stairway to Aunt Lou's house was at the end of the hallway at the rear of the house. We liked to play there on the landing where the stair turned and continued to the second floor. The turn in the stairway intrigued us and we approached it with awe as we did everything else that was strange to us. I was scared of the rooms above but my avid curiosity impelled me upward. I was the mouse who always tasted the cheese first and if a trap didn't snap shut on me, my sister Dorothy followed suit. So we climbed the stairs to the great unknown, with her about three steps behind me, where we peeked into the four rooms.

One room belonged to Aunt Lou's brother, the next two were empty, but the fourth room belonged to "her." She must have been about sixteen with beautiful white teeth, thick, dark, curly hair and a Jayne Mansfield-ish figure. The first time I saw her was the time I became aware of the difference between six and sixteen. I gaped in wide-eyed wonder at her and tried to imitate her by walking in front of the mirror with my fists thrust under my apron front. It was no good though, because the minute I removed them the illusion was gone and I was once again just plain, skinny, little me!

She was the first person I ever saw use toothpaste. She made quite a ritual of it by brushing and rinsing and brushing again. She must have thought us a couple of idiots the way we followed her around watching everything she did. She told us each to hold out a finger. Then she pressed a magic tube and out came a little worm of toothpaste for each of us. She said that it was good and for us to taste it. We did and it was good and I ate every bit of mine. We wanted Mama to buy us some, but she said it was just a pack of foolishness and that she had never had any. I didn't dare remind her that she didn't have any front teeth, either.

Marie's room was sunny and cheerful. She was a carefree and happy girl and I guess she would rather live with faded rugs than to shut out the beautiful sunshine. On her dresser were all sorts of sweet-smelling things. One time when we climbed the stairs she was in her room dressing and invited us in. It was fun to watch her because she went at her brushing and primping with the same enthusiasm as she did her toothbrushing, as though she were having the time of her life. She took what looked to me like a large round cookie, dipped it in a little black box, and patted it all over her face and neck. Then she took a smaller one and rubbed bright red all over her cheeks. She showed us her earrings which went right through her ears. I bawled for a week because Mama refused to pierce my ears so I could wear some. Out of one of the bottles, by squeezing a small rubber bulb, she sprayed perfume on her neck, her hair, her wrists and her hanky. Then with a swish and a flutter she was gone—the most beautiful and best-smelling thing I had ever seen. She was no sooner out of the house than I dared to touch her comb. My sister looked on in horror as I tried to arrange my hair in buns over my ears. Wanting so desperately to be like cousin Marie, I threw caution to the wind and set to with the powder puff, the rouge and the perfume bottle. I thought I had done a good job of it and swished my dress tail going downstairs to meet an imaginary beau. When my mother saw me she almost fainted with embarrassment but my entire Aunt Lou shook with laugher.

Mama was so mortified by my behavior that she bid Aunt Lou a hasty farewell, bundled the two of us in the buggy, whacked old Nellie a good one on the rump and took off for home like greased lightning! She forgot all about "lathering" old Nellie, but I knew she was concentrating on who was going to get "lathered" when we got home. It didn't bother me much because I was blissfully munching sugar cookies, listening to the rhythmic clop, clop of Nellie's feet, watching the neat tracks the rubber-tired wheels made in the dust, and wishing we could go "over to Aunt Lou's" every single day!

This Is How I Remember Mama

I remember many things about my childhood. About my sister next to me and the younger two who followed. I remember Papa as he was long ago, but when I think of our little home south of Markle, here's how I remember Mama.

I remember her by the cherry tree with a soft breeze playing hide and seek in her long skirts as she reached out to fill her pail with cherries.

I remember what she baked that morning—rich brown cookies sprinkled white with sugar. I remember Mama thought she'd filled our hunger before she left us, but we thought differently we two, and as soon as Mama was safely out of sight we helped ourselves to more good cookies. I remember Mama calling through the open window, "I'll know if you girls eat more cookies, I counted them, you know!" I remember the look upon my sister's face and our hasty consultation, and how I hurried to the knife drawer. With the sharpest knife I found there I slice through many cookies to replace the ones we'd eaten. Then I camouflaged deception with a heavy coat of sugar. I remember, too, that we just *thought* that we'd fool Mama!

I remember Mama in the rocking chair with its wide arms. It was summer and she brought it to a bare spot in the side yard. My sister carried our new hymnbook. Mama rocked and sang with a little girl perched on each arm beside her. I remember looking westward. It was evening and the trees there danced against a backdrop of watermelon sky!

I remember too, this same old rocker by the fireside where Papa pressed me to his bosom while Mama mixed a potion to relieve my croup or earache. I remember how secure I felt there as I listened to his heartbeat, and his rough hand stroked away my headache.

I remember Mama when she had her hair bobbed. I tried to sew the tresses to a headband. I wondered how I'd look if I had long, dark hair like Mama's. I remember how I also sewed my finger and how scared I was until I took my hurt to Mama.

I remember one hot summer evening my sister watched while I gave both our cats a haircut. We saved the hair in Papa's hat that he would wear to work the next morning. I remember Mama laughing, but Papa didn't think it was funny.

I remember Mama sewing. How she fashioned all our clothing from shapeless piles of yardage. I remember very often when time was short she sewed into the night by lamplight.

I remember Mama at her dough board. I remember my deep hunger when that rare aroma emanated from the oven! How I remember that thick slice of fresh, warm bread coated with our homemade butter and sprinkled with brown sugar!

I remember Mama preparing for the winter, canning all the surplus our garden could afford. Drying corn and apple slices, making kraut and apple butter, picking beans to shell before the open oven door. She gathered nuts and gleaned the popcorn, and helped to store the apples in their bin. She wrapped the yams and hung pulled onions up to dry. Then she carried in the pumpkins that ended up in golden pie. All the while I helped her we would talk. She would answer all my questions; tell me things I ought to know. She was much more than my mother—she was my everlasting friend!

I remember Mama on my first day of school. How she walked with me the mile, then I went on alone. I remember at the door I turned and found her there still watching as I choked back my tears and entered my new world!

I remember still and pray to reassure her as she did me that day when I walk with her on her last mile. When our hands again unclasp and she walks on alone, may my presence there beside her help *her* through the door to her world yet unknown!!

Yes, I remember many things about my childhood, about my sister next to me and the younger two who followed. I remember Papa as he was long ago, but most of all when I recall our little home south of Markle, this is how I remember Mama!!

For Wildcat Days

What would they think today—those sturdy pioneers who pushed north and west to find better lives for themselves and their children?

Would Mr. and Mrs. Yesterday quake in their shoes if we were to tell them an American flag had been planted on the moon, and explain to them how it got there? Would they believe us if we told them we had watched it happen through the media of television?

Could they comprehend the almost incomprehensible idea that years could be added to men's lives through the skill and knowledge of heart surgeons or that childhood diseases have almost been eliminated?

Could they possibly fathom the miracles that Edison's light bulb loosed on the world or that the John Deere or McCormick inventions could gobble up in a few hours acres and acres of grain which took them weeks or months to harvest?

But—would they trade their security gained little-by-little and year-by-year for the insecurity of our securities?

Would they trade the worry of finding something to cook in the pot to feed their children for the "pot" that destroys the lives and minds of our children? Would they trade the implications of the old musket that hung over the door for the fear of a war where nobody wins?

Would they trade the simplicity of their religion for the cults and Satanism we read about with fear and trembling?

Would they trade their togetherness in establishing a home and raising a family for the struggle young people endure in this day of progress and enlightenment where it takes two wage-earners to even begin to think of owning a home and paying the bills incurred in the maintenance of that home?

Our little town, like the world, has seen many changes—many good and many not so good. Its growth has been an uphill battle, but it has made it over the hill and is spreading in all directions.

We must remember that it isn't the quantity of growth but the quality that decides our future happiness. We must struggle to maintain family unity, to work together in harmony and like our forefathers, remember the God who made it all possible!

The Dress

I hate to shop for clothes, but occasionally a need arises and it is imperative that I drag myself to town to buy a new dress.

Such an occasion arose about three years ago when a granddaughter announced she was getting married. I didn't need to look in my closet for something suitable to wear because I knew if I were to take everything in it to the Goodwill they would reject it!

I gave every shop for miles around the privilege of selling me a new dress, but none of them stocked anything in the right dimensions! Everything was down to the floor or up to mid-thigh or too narrow—hardly appropriate for a seventy-nine-year-old grandmother!

As usual, after an exhaustive search, I found one! It was very plain with a round neck and a narrow belt. My friend and the clerk convinced me that with suitable jewelry it would be beautiful. It did fit and was sort of cute in the back. It was cut a little lower than the front with four tiny buttons. Thank heavens, I wouldn't have to fool around with a back zipper!

There are so many things to occupy ones mind in the spring. A house to clean, garden to tend, yard to care for and a host of other things that take one's mind off of what one is going to look like at a wedding.

The day arrived and after one last look I decided I looked pretty "snazzy."

The church was beautiful, my darling granddaughter was beautiful, the groom was handsome, the flowers were gorgeous and I was grateful for a plain dress because it didn't distract from the beauty of my corsage. The ceremony was beautiful and when it was over Mr. and Mrs. Charles Vernon walked down the aisle amid the best wishes from us all.

During the reception I kept tugging at my dress. It didn't really feel comfortable and the horrible thought came to me that I must have put on a few pounds during the three weeks it hung in the closet!

The next Sunday "The Dress" and I went to church. Over a cup of coffee afterwards the thing bugged me so badly I decided to turn it around, because it was lower in the back and might not threaten to strangle me. "If it feels better that way, I'll just wear it backward," I said to myself.

It sure felt better and the horrible, shocking realization came to me that I—at last—had it on right!

Erma Bombeck once gave this advice to the mother of the groom: "Wear beige and keep your mouth shut!"

My advice to this grandmother for the next wedding is to "wear black and sit in the back!"

This short story was written for the week
that I attended a college writing course.

Precious Interlude

In early August I was awakened by the loud honking of geese. Grabbing my housecoat and fumbling for the snaps, I tore out the door to behold the panorama of a beautiful V formation in the sky. I stood rooted to the spot as I watched them disappear flying in perfect unison. I stood for a long time looking upward and noticed how very blue the sky was and how very white the clouds that floated against it! Then I noticed pink edges on them and realized the sun was beginning to appear above the horizon. In a matter of seconds it seemed an artist had splashed color over all the clouds for they were a delicate pink. I looked around me enthralled with the beauty of the earth. The grass was as green as in springtime, the flowers were dewy with morning freshness, the robins were searching for breakfast, and a pair of doves were cooing to each other between the pine tree and the electric power line! How incredibly beautiful! If this tiny spot of earth can be so beautiful, what must Heaven be like! What joy and beauty must my loved one be experiencing! As I stood there refreshed in body and soul I began to look forward again! These thoughts rushed through my mind, and it was as if someone spoke to me and said, "My child, I'm putting you down now. It's time for two pairs of footprints in the sand. You must walk again but not alone. I will always be beside you!"

For this precious interlude, I am indeed thankful.

How to Be a Good Mother-in-Law

*L*earning to be a good mother-in-law begins when ones first child is born. If he is taught to help himself and to shoulder responsibilities befitting his age, he will grow into the responsibilities of manhood and marriage. If his mother ties his shoelaces and wipes his nose for twenty years she needn't expect him to don manhood like a new coat.

The extended hand of welcome to her child's friends will set a pattern in his life from which all will benefit when he reaches manhood. The extended, friendly hand might very well be the trademark of a good mother-in-law.

The following words are good to remember, "But in the beginning of creation God made them male and female. For this cause shall a man leave his father and mother and cleave to his wife."—Bible. Only a weak minded fool would interfere with this great law by feeling flattered in having her son cleave to her rather than his wife!

Take time to look at yourself in relationship with your own mother-in-law. If it is good, try to emulate it in your relationship with your daughter-in-law. If otherwise, mark the pitfalls and avoid them.

Keep busy! There's always a spot where a flower will grow!

Make new friends, or dig up some old ones (except, of course those six feet under!) Don't expect your married children to parent-sit every night listening to a dull account of all your aches and pains!

BE HAPPY! Then you will find a smiling welcome anywhere!

The above statements are all time-tested and true!

I am top banana as a mother-in-law. My daughter-in-law told me so! I learned how to be from my husband's mother!

First Day

On this, my first day of college (?) I marvel at the knowledge of our Instructor. Will I ever be able to attain a semblance of what she possesses?

Reading is a mode of travel for one such as I, who have not been privileged to do much of it physically, but mentally can travel, by means of a good book, anywhere in the world and be home before the hungry family assembles for the evening meal!

Reading can lift one from dull routine, refresh one after a toilsome day.

My desire in hoping to write something worthwhile is to bring joy and happiness into the lives of others!

Untitled

When I go shopping I stare in amazement at the displays of toys and other paraphernalia that is supposed to entertain and educate our children. I guess we must have been terribly under privileged when we were kids, but we never realized it for we thoroughly enjoyed ourselves. What we lacked in substance we made up for in imagination. That, plus an avid curiosity left us little time with nothing to do.

We always had pet kittens. We cuddled, baptized them and gave them haircuts. When we tired of our dolls we dressed our cats. Once we purloined items from our baby sister's wardrobe to dress them in. My cat tired of these hijinks long before we did, slipped his moorings and ran under the corncrib! I tried to crawl under too, but there was no way as my circumference exceeded that of the cat several times. We called and called but that durned cat turned a deaf ear and it wasn't until we emerged dirty and distraught into the out-of-doors that we saw him sitting on a fence post grinning and licking his paw!

There were several mysteries in my mother's life and what happened to those baby clothes was one of them!

Another mystery happened one time after our dad announced he was taking us to Huntington to see our first airplane. For days afterward we could scarcely think of anything else. I climbed up into the apple tree with mom's eggbeater and flew all over the countryside! My sister was afraid to climb up into the tree, so she made her flying debut running as fast as she could while turning the eggbeater. She didn't get far enough off the ground and failed to see the rock she fell over. When my turn came to fly again, the propeller was jammed and I realized that was nothing compared to the "jam" we would be in when Mom saw her egg beater, so we pounded it out with a rock the best we could and slipped it back into the drawer.

One of the great highlights of our young lives was when a new catalog came for we were allowed the old one to play with. All the shiny pages were ours for the family had a use for the ones that could be softened by crumpling.

We hastened to cut out pictures of men, women and children so we could get started on our long journey across the ocean. Our favorite game was the Pilgrims crossing the Atlantic. We cried when we left our "Father Land" and chilled when the storms beset us on our journey across the dangerous expanse, which was the dining room floor. When we landed, our wild screams at the sight of Indians brought out Mother from the kitchen to see what in the world was going on! When she saw we weren't killing each other her comment was usually, "Better get that mess cleaned up before your dad gets home!" We made the perilous trip so often that our paper dolls were worn out, as the real travelers must have been.

Our parents planted a large garden every spring and we were always on the spot to help. Once (when I think they were trying to get rid of us) Dad marked off a little space and told us we could plant our own garden. "What can we plant?" was our first question. "Whatever you like best," was the answer. So we quickly planted *Pearl Tapioca*!

My favorite hide-away was up among the leaves in the cherry tree in the front yard. My sister had no patience with anyone who sat around with her nose in a book, so that's where I liked to read and look and listen. When I got old enough to have access to the school library I brought home books, which my mother and I read and discussed. We also played writing games and sometimes stayed up until almost nine o'clock! Did you know that you can make twenty-seven or more words from the word "Markle"? Now I know that is no earth-shaking discovery, but these games were a great source of entertainment, a source of close relationship between my mother and I, and a means of learning to concentrate. All the things we did were pretty tame compared to the means of amusement kids have now. I have seen children with a room full of toys wonder what to do and if they are given a cardboard carton, a piece of string, and an idea, they are busy and happy for a long time. The thing is that although they may have created an unsightly mess, this treasure they have designed and built must remain where it is until it self-destructs, because their pride of accomplishment cannot be taken lightly.

We were lucky enough to have chores to do, although we didn't consider ourselves lucky then. Besides the every day chores, it was my job to help my dad when he needed me. I rode the horse when he plowed the garden, turned the grind stone when he sharpened things, held the rope when he tied fodder shocks, helped him husk corn, put the rings in the clamp when it was time to put rings in the pigs noses, hold the sack when he sacked grain, and filled in for the son he didn't have on many occasions. One job I dearly loved was herding the cow along the road when the pasture in the field was short! My sister was drafted to do the mundane things in my absence and I was off with the old cow and my favorite book. I was never bored with this job because the wind kept me company as I read or watched the clouds in the summer sky. There was always an ant going some place or a bug crawling around that gave me food for thought for a long time.

When the cow had her fill I reluctantly took off for home where I pumped water to alleviate her thirst. That was one of the jobs I didn't care for in the wintertime. The pump had no protection and I nearly froze because on her diet of dry hay she required a lot of water. I complained to my mother about my cold hands and she told me that was nothing compared to what she heard had happened to someone she knew. Seems that this person had stuck his tongue on the frosty pump handle and nearly pulled it out! "For pity sakes don't every try that" was her admonishment. Well guess what! Somebody did, somebody was sorry and somebody was mighty glad to get loose without having to call for help. Somebody has often been told that it's a pity that more of the offended member didn't stick fast to the pump handle.

You know, looking back over the years I believe life would have been easier for our mother and less hazardous for us if we could have punched a button in front of the TV and let the little characters on Atari, etc., take all the chances, but I know it wouldn't have been half so much fun!

Poetry

Markle, Indiana

There's a certain fascination to places far away
But after you've seen them, I have only this to say
It is great to seek adventure, and finding it is fine
But there's no place comparable with this hometown of mine.
It started with one cabin a long, long time ago
When this was Indian country and white man was his foe
It spilled across the Wabash and climbed up o'er the hill,
It boasted of a blacksmith and of a flourmill.
The old hotel is gone now, the old tie barn, the harness shop
The photo gallery, the creamery, the ice cream parlor where we
loved to stop
Many souls have come and gone, its founders lie at rest,
In the peaceful little garden on the hilltop to the west.
It is lovely in the springtime, to stroll along the county line
And look down on the housetops in this little town of mine.
To see the yards and gardens, to smell the earth at morn
To hear the robins singing makes me glad that I was born.
It is pleasant in the summer at our town's swimming pool
When half the population is bent on keeping cool.
It is magic in the autumn when the streets are paved with gold
After Jack Frost nips the maples and the nights are getting cold
It's a Christmas card in winter when flakes of icy down
Change the color and the contour of everything in town.
It's a picture of contentment when the snow lies deep and white
To see the lighted windows, shine out through the night.
Then and only then nostalgia stings my eyes with unshed tears
I'd relive those winter evenings could I turn back the years.
I'd love to hear my children's laughter, the scraping sleds, the
stamping feet.

To watch them eat a hearty supper, then tuck them in for slumber sweet.
City folks are good folks too, but it's my town I hold dear
'Cause I know if I've a heartache my whole town will shed a tear.
I can be myself and they still love me for when the chips are down
You really can't fool anyone that lives in my hometown.
Life is great in my hometown, but there will come a day
When I shall have to leave it because I cannot stay.
If I could have my "druthers" then it is my will
To sleep beside the river with my town folks on the hill.

Grandma's Christmas Tree

There's a glorious something in the air
You can sense it's Being everywhere
The world is getting its self in tune
To celebrate a birthday coming soon

Goodies are made and stored away
To await the coming of the great day
And grandma's as busy as she can be
When it's time to trim the Christmas tree

It begins with a star at the very tip-top
Then strings of lights from the electric shop
Then the tinsel, the beads, and icicles too
Grandmother never quite knows when she's through

In the boxes of trim she digs all around
Some forgotten items are sure to be found
She pulls them all out and then one by one
She recalls everything under the sun!

Ah! The memories on tree trimming day!
How many there are it is hard to say!
Love and devotion garland every limb there
And over it all a canopy of prayer!

Thanksgiving for gifts that are felt and not seen
For births, mellow aging and years in between!
So much hangs there that no one can see
After Grandma has trimmed her Christmas tree!

My Cross

My CROSS was growing heavy,
    Far too much to bear,
I cried beneath its burden,
    Then someone found me there,
He raised my CROSS to free me,
    And pointed out the way
That I could raise my own CROSS
    Should it return someday.
In haste to do the bidding
    Of that dear voice so sweet
I knelt, and then I saw them,
    The nail prints in his feet.
I prayed and lo, my CROSS began
    To change and break apart,
I found the peace I long had sought
    For my troubled aching heart,
When I arose no longer there
    The CROSS that burdened me,
I found instead an alter
    And I at last was free,
All my CROSSES large or small
    On the alter now I lay,
And find that they will disappear
    While I kneel there and pray.

From a Thankful Mother

The day with its cares, is over
My children are clean and fed.
Their daddy is deep in the sport pages
I plant a kiss on each dear head.

One is auburn like my own
Freckles pepper an upturned nose
I know God hears his "Now I lay me"
As the lids of his blue eyes close.

Of the dark little head, I love each curl
I cherish the imps in the big round eyes
God hears my prayer, for my little girl
As she, snugly by her brother lies

The other dark head is flecked with gray
I love the lines in the tired face
I ask God to help him on his way
With faith and truth to run the race

For one who hold these three so dear
Understanding and patience I pray
Then closing my eyes, I whisper "How sweet
Is love—and the end of day."

~Written in 1941 for Jerry and Linda

To a Dear Friend

Both children are gone from the country nest
One on the east coast, one on the west.
Did Edith sit down on her tail and cry?
I guess she didn't! She learned to fly!

She's been to London to look at the queen
She's the "flyingest" person I've ever seen!
She's been to Hawaii, she didn't say so
But I think she went just to see Don Ho!

I wonder if she has ever boarded a plane
And passed the first time in the safety check lane?
When they open her luggage to take a look
They find the metal object is a crochet hook!

Like the Travelers Express card, no doubt about it
She would never, never leave home without it.
There might even be a needle or two
In case she finds some quilting to do!

My purple martin, in confidence one day
Said a red bird out flew him on his way
To the land of Sunshine, but later he found
It was a new Ford flying low to the ground!

Know who was driving? Of course you know
A white haired lady escaping the snow
She goes south, she goes east and west—who knows
She may spend next winter with the Eskimos!

Where ever she goes I know there'll be friends
For her hospitality never ends
All summer long her house is open
Family and friends drop by just hopin'
For an old fashioned home-cook meal
Back on the farm where life is real.

And at night when they climb upstairs to their beds
My! What her pillows can do for tired heads!
She is everything that a mother should be
No question about, and take it from me
As a friend she is kind, considerate and gracious
And holds each friend as a jewel most precious.

So hang in there and keep flying, dear Lady
You aren't old just because you are eighty
I make a promise—when you're a hundred and two
I'll try to write a better poem for you.

~Happy Birthday From Alfreda
Written for Edith Priebble

The Coming of the Flowers

I walked today, in my flower garden
But there were no flowers in bloom
Only the bushes and vines did I see
I caught no sweet perfume.

I did not linger long, but as I went
I heard a noise by the garden walk
I listened and lo, it was a rose bush
Just beginning to talk.

I listened to its soft, sleepy voice
Here is what it said,
"Oh Easter lily, open your eyes
And awaken the violet from her bed."

"Awaken Sweet William, too
Get Jack in his pulpit today."
The green leaves of the rose bush came out
And welcomed the sweet air of May.

"Tell the cherry tree to arise
And throw off her wintry gown
Tell her to dress in her spring attire
Of blossoms as soft as down."

All these things the rose bush said
Then I went away
But I returned not long afterwards
And gathered a beautiful, fragrant bouquet.

~Written in the spring—early spring of 1927.
  Alfreda Dennis at the age of 17

The Dreamer

The dreamer dreams such wonderful dreams
As he dreams the hours through
I know he dreams, of what he dreams
For I'm a dreamer too.

The dreamer dreams of the-might-have-beens
He dreams of what is past
He dreams of the most impossible things.
From the first of his dreams to the last.

He builds air castles that touch the sky
Round them sweet dream flowers grow
Each petal is a dream gone by
A dream of the long ago.

Picture of childhood days now gone
Adorn his castle walls,
Sounds of dear voices hushed so long
Ring through his castles halls.

Each stone in his castle is a dream
A hope for the very best
Disturb him not in this his home
His house of dreams, his place of rest.

~Hilda Alfreda Dennis, age 17

Pussy Willow

Dainty Pussy-Willow
Blowing in the breeze
Air is rather chilly
Aren't you 'fraid you'll freeze?

Brave Pussy-Willow
Shakes her head "No, No,
Winter's gone and Springtime
Has driven away the snow."

Saucy Pussy-Willow
Tosses her pretty head.
"Mother Nature said 'arise'
And I am here," she said.

~ Written after gathering Pussy-Willows with which to decorate the
reception room at Markle in honor of the Seniors of twenty-eight.

Thanks from the Heart of Me!

I thank you, God, for eyesight
And all the joy it brings
When I behold your handiwork
My heart truly sings!

No artist yet has captured
True beauty of sunsets glow
Or ever blended on his canvas
But an imitation rainbow!

Through all the gorgeous colors
That beautify this earth of ours
I'm reminded of your greatness
When I behold the flowers.

The green and blue of earth and sky
The golden ripeness of the grain
The white of clouds and fallen snow
The silver sparkle of the rain –

The gray and black of noble trees
Silhouetted in the west
Against a mauve back drop of evening
Remind me how my life is blessed.

The rust and scarlet piles of fun
Where children romp and play
Are things of joyous beauty
On a golden autumn day.

The earth is filled with beauty
For the whole wide world to see
And I am getting my share
With these eyes you gave to me.

May my fervent love of nature
Reach out to all mankind
But when I behold my brother
Lord, make me color blind!

To a New Little Boy

And so a little boy
Has come to bless you two
To bring you joy and dirt and laughter
And a way of life you never knew.

Skinned knees and sunshine
Just picture if you can
An appetite to marvel at
In such a little man.

Washer loads of grimy clothes
Pockets yielding a worm, a string
You'll wonder where he finds it all
He won't miss anything.

His innocence and dependency
Will strike cords you never knew you had
When he waves his arms and kicks his feet
And smiles at mom and dad.

To Don

This is a jug
To keep in the trunk
Of the little blue Ford
That Don bought

This is a cork
To fit in the jug
To keep in the trunk
Of the little blue Ford
That Don bought

This is some gas
To dampen the cork
To fit in the jug
To keep in the trunk
Of the little blue Ford
That Don bought

This is some dough
To pay for the gas
To dampen the cork
To fit in the jug
To keep in the trunk
Of the little blue Ford
That Don bought

To Rich

Boys get neckties and socks
And belt sets and shirts
And so many cuff links
That he actually hurts!

The shirts are too big
And the socks are too small
The cuff links so gaudy
That he's sick of it all!

Now he has a good friend
And he'd rather by far
That folks give him green stuff
To feed his old car!

So here's a few bucks
To buy her some hay
To go out and make whoopee!
On Graduation Day!

~Written for Rich Anderson

Farewell to Summer

Like a miser
Hoards the gold
Of an autumn afternoon
To cheer me through the gray days
Of the winter coming soon

I store the pleasant memories
Of October's gentle breeze
I know it will sustain me
During winters' icy freeze.

I'll remember all the flowers
When the cold winds blow
And know they're sweetly resting
Just beneath the snow.

I'll remember silvery stands
Visible against the sun
And the thought will surely cheer me
After winter has begun.

To Shirley

You mean so much to both of us
And on this special day
We'll try to find the words
For the things we'd like to say

Our family circle, far more dear
Than any other earthly thing
Is dearer for you being here
With all the gifts you bring.

Gifts of love for one we love
Our own beloved son
The home you make, the pride you take
In having things well done.

Your greatest gift, two angels
For on our family tree
To bring us joy, and girl and boy
Happiness for Dad and Me.

A Modern Thanksgiving

From freezer and cupboard
Grandma took a survey
Of all the things stashed there
For Thanksgiving Day

Oven ready turkey roll
Resplendent in foil
Creamed peas and carrots
All ready to boil.

Cranberry relish there
Waiting to thaw
Also corn on the cob
Just to please Pa!

There's luscious Cool Whip
For "Wicks" pumpkin pies
Pop cycles and ice cream
For the kids big surprise

Then she went to the cupboard
Which was far from bare
Instant pudding and cake mix
Were plentiful there.

Pickles, olives and relishes
Red apple rings too
Instant mashed potatoes
Plenty for a hungry crew.

Then she called Grandpa
From his couch in the den
"Do you know Thanksgiving
Has rolled 'round again?"

The kids are all coming
Our family's getting big!
But the heat from the oven
Might damage my wig.

I mustn't break down
On my weight-watchers diet
I'll fall to temptation
I'm afraid, if I try it.

You know I'm a weakling
There isn't a doubt
I'll get reservations
And you can take us all out!

Mom's Pumpkin Pie

I could smell it from my bedroom
Or when outdoors at play
Or when the school bus brought me home
At the end of a long school day.

No one ever needed to tell me
What my mother did that day or why
My own built-in smell-a-vision
Said, "Boy, there's pumpkin pie!"

My legs were slow to carry me
Where my nose was pointing to
I'd nearly fall inside the door
Just to get a first hand view.

A piece of pie and ice cold milk
Made coming home so sweet
Cake and cookies both are good
But pumpkin pie's a treat!

Dear Elmer:——

I will see you in the morning
Where the day is always new
When my time on earth is over
I will come to you.

I do not question God's decision
For you to go while I must stay
He will give the strength I need
To look beyond today.

Walking eternally side by side
We will understand his plan
Sweet memories will comfort me
'Til I see you again.

~Love Alfreda

Gifts from Small Hands

Darling little grandchild
With your gifts of gold
Overflowing chubby handsful
You don't know what you hold.

You praise your lovely mother
Many times a day;
You give her adoration,
In your dandelion bouquet.

Though she may receive an orchid
Or a rose corsage or two
She'll not remember one of them
Like this dandelion from you.

Getting Old

The joy of growing old
Are the memories stored away
And you count them like rare jewels
Some time when you say.
Do you remember? Yes, I do.
And the moments go flying by
Recollections bring forth laughter
But sometimes you cry.

I open one eye
If I like what I see
I open the other
Then flex one knee

I reach for my glasses
To look for my teeth
Feel all over the bed
Find them underneath

With both feet on the floor
I stretch and I yawn
Then fall back in bed
And let time just pass on.

Back Yard U.S.A. (song)

There are bands of soldiers strong and brave
Marching up and down
They're training for the Navy's blue
And for the Army's brown.

They neither look to the right nor left
Each carries a heavy gun
I know that these big brave marines
Have the Japanese on the run.

I hear ack-ack from morn 'til night
From the fox holes all around
A curly top gives candy pills
To the wounded on the ground.

I hear instructions shouted loud
They're off with an awful din
I know that my back yard Air Force
Is off to bomb Berlin.

Life

All the world's not decked with flowers
But sunshine always follows showers.
If you wait, you'll not wait in vain,
For sunshine and gladness follows rain.
If sorrows clouds around you hang
Try to be happy, try to sing.
Look forward to the coming day
When these dark clouds have passed away.
Oh, that day when your prize is won
You'll be glad for the good you've done.
Whatever may come, or whatever may go
Maybe 'tis best that it should be so.
So remember—life's not all flowers
Or dreams in shady nooks and bowers.
But 'tis just a waiting place
'Til death comes for us to face
Then we'll be happy on the other shore
Where heartbreaks and partings shall be no more.

~Hilda Alfreda Dennis at the age of 16—
  sorrowing for an old friend.

To Be a Child Again

Many years have passed since John and Jim
Together listened to an old, old hymn
At the Sunday School in the maple grove
Where lazy smoke idled from a potbelly stove

They didn't hear much the teacher said
Their eyes peered through the door instead
To a far away hill where spring with glee
Had left a thousand new things to see

Two boys who loved to spend their hours
Discovering new rocks, trees and flowers
So strange that they to men should grow
And forget these things they used to know

Now Jim lives on his father's farm
He cuts the wood that keeps him warm
There should be memories, but instead a frown
For this, just another tree cut down

He sees his far fields growing green
And boasts," They're the richest fields I've seen."
He forgets how with John and the spotted pups
There he once raced to find spring buttercups.

John in a far away city stands
With a highball glass in his idle hands
From his richly draped window he seems to see
A picture of life as he'd wish it to be

His costly gardens fail to imitate
The riot of flowers at his mother's gate
Even though they did, there'd be no hill
Where a boy could gallop away at will

So John, having gold realizes his loss
Jim seeking wealth, bears such a cross
That he looks at only with unseeing eyes
The beauties of nature that John would prize

John, disillusioned, choked on his gold
Finds wealth a burden. It does not hold
All the magic he'd dreamed of a long time before
When he envied the rich men who passed by his door

Jim restless, unhappy seeks for the place
That John would give gladly could he erase
The years and again be a carefree lad
Tagging along by the side of his dad

Both grown men, successful it seems
Yet each one, envious, of the other dreams
God, recall childhood to the memory please
Of this man at work, and this man at ease

Strike it Rich

School bus leads you to water
But he cannot make you drink
Teacher makes the day so pleasant
But she cannot make you think!

Cooky smiles and is so cheerful
As she dishes up the stew
Whether or not you eat it
Is strictly up to you!

School presents the nutriments
Of which you need to grow
Cooky, gastronomically
Teacher, what you ought to know

So hunger after learning
You'll starve just sitting still
"Thar's gold in them thar textbooks"
You can find it if you will!

There'll be rock and stumbling blocks
But the lodes worth digging for
You will find before you reach it
Tons and tons of useless ore

Untitled

At a bake sale you bake it
You give it, you buy
You really give twice
So this year we'll try
A less troublesome way

We ask you to give us
A "buck" or a "fin"
For a bakeless bake sale
And when it's all in
We hope it will pay

Our letters will reach
Both those near and far
Is it too much trouble
For your Eastern Star?
To send something today?

You know any donation
We will gladly receive
And in the long run
We really believe
We can truthfully say

We've made it much easier
There are "no ifs" or "butts"
We've saved your raisins and sugar
Gas, flour and nuts
And you have helped O.E.S. on its way.

To Suzette

Worthy Matron, I have brought you
A pretty pink bouquet
A bouquet of lovely roses
I just picked along the way

Roses have a way of saying
Words my tongue falter on
May their message still ring clearly
When this nightlong has gone

Roses are God's earthly symbols
Of the love Christ died to give
And if in faith we mortals share it
Harmony rules these lives we live

Love has a way of growing greater
The more it's shared the more it grows
The world's insatiable hunger
Could find fulfillment in a rose.

If our faith is real, our love undaunted
We may reach the plan here below
Of exaltation through privation
The highest reward Earth can bestow

One by one the fragile petals
In their falling now disclose
What we've hoped to keep a secret
Hidden in our center rose

Someone very near and dear
Bears your chapter's gift to you
Receive it with our fondest wishes
Which go with you all year through

To Howard

Bright golden mornings are just ahead
Because Howard won't have to climb out of bed
Or bolt down a bite and be on his way
To start the wheels turning for another day

He can punch his old pillow, snuggle down in his nest
Eat breakfast at noon without getting dressed
He can throw that alarm clock as far as he can
Or let it scream its head off for the garbage man

He can rest on his laurels or hop on a plane
Take a slow boat or catch a mule train
He can drive his own car, or take a sight seeing bus
When he gets tired of roaming, he can come home to us

We'll all be here, still slaving away
Envying him and awaiting the day
When we can leisurely walk up and down
Saying "Hi" and "Good Morning" to every body in town

If he goes all out and has quite a bash
And comes back home a little short of cash
His qualifications are very well known
So the State Bank of Markle will grant him a loan.

Remember?

Do you remember
How in golden September
We gathered with old friends once more?
How we laughed, how we talked
How proudly we walked
Once again toward the old school house door?

Let's go back for a while
With a tear and a smile
To recall the days in the time of "when"
Ah that we might forgive
And live and let live
Like we did as children then!

On that first day
Recall the bouquet
Of little girls in delicate hues?
The impish eyed boys
Some sneering, some poised
Some embarrassed in squeaky new shoes?

Remember the fun
As we one by one
Found our seats as "he" called each name?
How we quaked when he spoke
Yet it seemed such a joke
How funny small nothings became.

How industriously we
While the master could see
Plied ourselves to the task then at hand
How our hearts yearned
For his back to be turned
In the good old days, weren't they grand?

No grander were they
Than this pleasant day
When it fades and belongs to the past
If we glean all the gold
These fun hours hold
To treasure and forever hold fast.

No power on this earth
Since the first man's birth
Can stay one moment in its winged flight
May we then live it
Do our utmost to give it
That to make it a memory bright

Symphony of September

Golden days of late September
To recall when bleak winds howl
Golden beauty to remember
Nights with Jack Frost on the prowl.

Find surprises left by him
Painted leaves in gorgeous hues
May my minds eye ner grow dim
Ner this precious moment lose.

Silver strands against the sun
Spiders seeking homes abroad
Fairy fingers one by one
Scatter leaves along the road

The drying corn and pumpkin vine
Testify to summers close
Chatting birds on tension line
In the garden not one rose.

On proud display the evergreen
Dares the frost and coming cold
She knows she'll be the "beauty queen"
When the rest of earth is brown and old.

Mingled with the golds and reds
Pink and purple asters flare
Showy mums, late sleepy heads
Vibrant beauty everywhere.

Fat crickets in their hideout doors
Serenade with last refrain
Ere they retire mid winter stores
To wait for spring to come again

All God's creatures join the song
Bringing joy to the heart of man
A great symphony that moves along
In perfect tune with God's great plan.

How great are they, how small am I!
For oft rebellion fills my soul
At tedious tasks which round me lie
Forgetting that God is in control.

They question not, while to querulous I
God patiently answers o'er and o'er
My frantic calls of why oh why!
My selfish cry for more and more.

I'll tune my life and then when I
Hear nature's great crescendo swell
Like autumn leaves lie down to die
And in my soul, find all is well.

To Ray Line

He never was needed when the weather was warm
    And a guy could enjoy a nice long ride.
But just let it get down to twenty below
    Or the snow shoulder deep outside!

Then his darned telephone would ring day and night!
    Grasshoppers who danced all summer were cold!
"We need some oil, and we want it right now!
    "We want it yesterday!" he often was told.

So good Sir Ray with his tank full
    That gallant, fearless, chivalrous knight
Would ride anywhere, anytime, any day
    To rescue any maiden from frostbite.

Doc Ray on his intervenes wagon
    Was a blessing to our neighborhood
He knew each sick and hungry furnace
    And all its ills he understood!

If you laid your hand upon old furnace
    And his brow was cold as ice
And this throat was black instead of red
    It was pretty dog gone nice

To know just whom to call upon
    In the sunshine or the rain
Who could pump life-giving fluid
    In old burners empty vein!

Now, you say that he's retiring?
        They're putting him upon the shelf?
Just be sure that it's well padded
        So he can sit and rest himself!

Cause he surely must have saddle-sores
        For all the years he rode "Old Red"
Now he deserves the best in comfort
        Deserves to loaf in the years ahead!

Sometimes when that red truck streaks by
        He'll leap up in his rocking chair
And try to beat it to the corner
        But he'll still be just sitting there!

He'll learn in time now nice it is
        And he's really got it made
When other guys are drenched in sweat
        And he is rocking in the shade!

On Calvary's Dark Hill

On Calvary's dark hill
A cross once stood
Chaffing my Lord
With its rough-hewn wood.

While bearing the scorn
Of a belligerent foe
He looked with compassion
On those weeping below.

From his pale, tortured face
The sweat poured down
And a blue flower grew
Where it watered the ground.

One golden sunbeam
Fell to earth that day
And a jasmine grew
In the light of its ray.

The pureness of heart
Of a few gathered there
Caused a lily to grow
While, graceful and fair.

The fern, emblem of life
Midst the sorrow and pain
Breathed its message unnoticed
In that rugged terrain.

Washed in his blood drops
From the cross just above
The rose stands forever
A symbol of love.

His cross disappeared
A long time ago
Swallowed in victory
For us here below.

The flowers still blossom
And even today
In the heart of the Godly
Can be found his bouquet

Sonnet to a Girl

Once you were such an elegant creature
Ah, girl, my poor heart it did all but stop
I had even considered contacting a preacher
Then one day I passed our town's beauty shop!

Your fragile beauty did so attract me
I could not but shake in my boots
Your bright golden halo did so distract me
I did not dream that it came from brown roots!

You are so fair, ah, fair as a rose
I had thought about changing your name
Now someone besides your hairdresser knows
And my love is no longer the same.

When I gaze into the depth of your eyes
Remembering these things my ardor dies.

~ Written for Rich Anderson for school poem

Sweet Memories

Sweet memories are golden threads
Through the fabric of our lives.
Speaking to us of the past
Binding us with joyful ties.

If we weave our fabric well
Avoiding snarls along the way
The gold will shine more brightly
On some distant far off day.

Untitled

One day I saw a little house
All white and green and new;
I loved that house for
I watched it as it grew.

I knew it in its infancy
Just a pile of boards and stone;
I also knew the master hand
Which helped it stand-alone.

I knew the wasp who with his trowel
Upon the chimney growing higher;
Did well his work that someone
Might have a cozy fire.

I knew the hand that beautified,
The artist at his trade;
And marveled that with just a brush
Such changes could be made.

I saw the card that read "For Sale",
Nailed where all might see;
And come to see the empty rooms,
In all their dignity.

Today I passed the little house,
Where curtained windows smiled;
I saw behind a picket fence,
A curly headed child.

Beside the fence I saw a man
Dig in the earth's soft brown;
I saw a mischief of a pup,
Scampering around.

I saw a lady neat and clean,
Mute evidence I own;
That one day I passed a little house;
Today I passed a home.

In Memoriam

The greatest memorial
To those who are gone
Is found in the lives
Of we who live on.

What of charity and love
They had to give
We can perpetuate
In the lives that we live.

The greatest legacy
To all mankind
Is by passing it on
To those left behind.

To forget human frailties
To ponder only the good
Joins us forever
In Christ's brotherhood.

A Lament on D.L.S.

It may not do any good at all
But I want to frame the clock on our wall.
Cause he's framed me, I think it a crime
How he caters to "Day Light Savings Time."

Early in spring he jumps 'way ahead
And I trot off wide-eyed to bed.
Makes no difference the fit I throw
"Clock" says I'm sleepy, so away I go.

Then comes the end of an autumn day
I'm dead tired so I head for the "hay"!
"Huh-uh" says mama, "Not for a while!"
And the face of the clock wears the silliest smile.

I think he's ashamed and full of disgrace
No wonder his hands are in front of his face
As I sit here droopy eyed and wait
For that dog-gone clock to say half past eight.

Our Secret

Come dear one, and let us go
Over the hill where the berries grow.
There with the shiny black caps to find
True enchantment, peace of mind.

Over the hill there's a little stream
Where we can dangle our feet and dream
Where we can open our hearts and share
The sadness and gladness hidden there.

There's a cool quiet glen at the foot of the hill
I knew as a child and remember it still
Where a deep, velvet moss carpet is laid
And boughs meet overhead to form a green shade.

There's a hush over all at the noon of the day
Tis nature's siesta. I will if I may
Pause to listen, and listening keep
Our rendezvous though she lies asleep.

There's fragrance all around and I'd dare
A perfumer to blend so exotic or rare
A sweetness as that which I know
Floats on the air as it did long ago.

Come dear one, let me share it with you
My beautiful secrets you will know too.
Then when one of us is forever still
The other in memory may go over the hill.

~Elmer gave this poem at my installation as Worthy Matron
of OES

Our Mom

She bore her cross with patience
Much like Christ at Calvary
In her lonely room she met Him
And He said, "Come, go with me!"

Once again the veil was lifted
And a dear soul took its flight
She was filled with understanding
As she passed beyond our sight.

All things now are clearer
Why our suffering, why our pain
Why God leads us through the valley
To reach that glorious plain.

My heart feels her message
Soothing, calming, bringing peace
And I know that I shall meet her
When this life on earth shall cease.

When she told me God was with her
My dearest wish came true
And my heart was filled with gladness
That her life on earth was nearly through
If she cast one backward glance
Or breathed a dying prayer
It was that all her children
Would one day meet her there.

With God's help we will meet her
In that world that needs no sun
Then we will fully comprehend
That our real life has just begun.

~ Written by Alfreda Mossburg in loving tribute to her mother,
Margaret Dennis. Born October 17, 1887. Died July 9, 1971.

A Poem—Alfreda Mossburg

A poem to a poet is
As oils on canvas to a painter are
As songs to a composers heart
As its reflection is to a star!

A poem is a deep emotion
Surging in the heart of me
Inadequate my tongue, I use
My pen to set it free.

A poem is a gift from God
Planted in this lump of clay
A fragment of my poet soul
To give to those along the way.

Life Measures

We measure our lifetime by minutes
Our food by the quart and the pound
We measure our distance by milestones
We even have measures for sound.

Our wealth is all measured by dollars and cents
We cook with the cup and the spoon
We measure the length and breadth of the earth
We know just the distance from here to the moon

With all of our knowledge of measures
One measure we cannot conceive
For tis boundless and knows no restrictions
Its vastness is hard to believe

Its seed is much smaller than atoms
But when planted in hearts of the wise
It mushrooms to gigantic proportions
And if properly fed never dies

There's no measure known for the heart and the soul
And for love no beginning or end
We can merely guess at its greatness
When we look in the face of a friend.

The Tree and the Vine

A sturdy old tree planted deep in the earth
Supported a vine that was frail and slim
By her understanding and life long love
She also protected him.

She softened the blows that life can give
And grew over the scars that he bore
Together they stood for many long years
And no one could ask for more.

Four young trees grew to womanhood
Sheltered with love and care
'Til they were reset beside young trees
In gardens far from there.

The tree and the vine inseparably grew
And the years bowed them down with pain
Still they clung together through it all
The sunshine and the rain.

Then the little vine withered and fell away
The old tree broken in heart and limb
Shed tears of anguish at the bier
And ask her to wait for him.

He kissed her and made his one last vow
"I'll meet you in Heaven" he said
And true to his word in nine short days
The broken old tree was dead.

Who was the stronger of the two
Yes, she was the first to pull free
But perhaps to prepare with her maker, a place
To welcome the broken old tree.

~Written by Alfreda Mossburg in loving tribute to her father,
* Alfred Dennis, Born May 2, 1883 and died July 18, 1971.*

Vast Heritage

How rich was I, a country child
Who played all day, and picked the wild
Sweet flowers which abundantly grew
In the beautiful wood where the sun shone thru!

Along Rock Creek in the Geiger wood
Where the simple home of an Indian once stood
My play mate and I whiled away happy hours
Where a dusky eyed maiden also picked flowers.

Perhaps in the spot where our play house stood
An Indian girl fashioned dollies of wood.
With a merry heart and the wind in her hair
Happy as we when we played there.

I wish these rocks might play back to me
The sounds here recorded of what used to be.
Faint whispers of lovers I seem to hear still
In the murmuring water, the wind on the hill.

Maybe here where I've chose to dream
A burdened woman came to rest by the stream
And when she arose from her torturous bed
Two overtook those who waited ahead.

Our acorn cups may have covered the grave
Which cradled the dust of an old Indian brave
Maybe in dying t'was his last desire
To rest near this stream by his own campfire.

I'd love to know what the old oak knows
Of those long ago summers and deep winter snows.
When he lived in peace before the pioneer craze
Broke his heart and his home with white man's ways.

The Farmer

Rich indeed is he who rises
Early with the morning sun
And as the infant day is being born
Sees his tasks well begun

He can hear the maestro tuning
For a concert all day long
He can hear the brown winged divas
Bursting into joyous song

In the east he sees the Master
Paint the backdrop for the day
Long before the sleepy actors
Are on stage to start the play

He can breathe in morning freshness
To invigorate his soul
He can understand more clearly
Just who is in control

Just whose hand runs the universe
That man, poor imitator
With all the great things he has done
Knows God has done them greater

He works with inspiration
And when his day is done
Lies down to peaceful slumber
He who rises with the sun

First Flight

All too soon my fledgling grew
To a full-grown bird. Then I knew
He'd soon be leaving his outgrown nest
For one of his own with her he loved best.

The branch they would choose, a long thin limb
Exposed to the sun and the fierceness of wind
Wasn't at all the place of my choice
But a wise mother bird never raises her voice.

Many the times I had risked a bad fall
From leaning to far out over the wall
Of my own nest, to admonish and advise
On how foolish were they, while I was so wise.

But there was something that I didn't see
And that was a little evergreen tree
It grew to a shelter, now in time of storm
They are cozy as I and as safe from harm.

~ Written for Jerry and Jean

Evening Chimes

Unmindful of the song they played,
I listened to the chimes dismayed;
That all day long I forgot to sing,
Had forgotten the joy that it could bring,

I raised my eyes to the west and lo!
On velvet cerise and indigo
A glittering gem displayed on high
To enrich the life of such as I.

Out of my soul the shadows flew,
Out of my heart a new song grew;
Out of the mouth a wordless prayer
As the chimes disappeared on the evening air.

June Day Storm

The wind came galloping through the wheat,
Rushed into town, down a busy street;
A Paul Revere of the coming storm,
Promised relief on June day warm.

Heat spent birds climbed again in the air
And finding refreshment they circled there;
They soared and tagged and again looked down
With wary eye on farmland and town.

Black, ominous clouds cut off the sun,
Spoiling his act before it was done;
Changing the scene and setting the stage,
For the lightening and thunder to vent their rage.

Bright half-dollar polka dots of rain
Spattered the walks while the weather vane;
Proud, saucy creature perched in the sky,
Defied the element threatening on high.

But this show off, tough boy the storm,
Harbored a heart that was gentle and warm;
For after it came the sweet summer rain,
Quenching the thirsty old earth again.

The anointed tree bent low its head
Sharing raindrops with the flowerbed.
The rose bush drank as never before,
But the peony reclined to rise no more.

All around the jeweled grass
Dampens the feet of those who pass;
To gaze in wonder that all too soon,
The rain cleaned house on a day in June.

Hide-a-way

In a secret chapel in my heart,
An altar's hidden there.
Secure from prying eyes and minds,
I lose myself in prayer.

I have no certain time a day,
No man made spot to kneel
When I turn my emotive soul
And ask of him to heal.

My world is tinged with sorrow now,
I try to hide my tears.
And hope they'll wash away the gloom
That threatens coming years.

When my darling is gone from me,
I'll countless times a day.
Camouflage him with my prayers
From my secret hide-a-way.

While hidden there, my strength will come
Direct from God to me.
My fears will die, my faith will grow,
My soul find liberty.

Little Brown House

Little brown house stands holding its breath
Wondering what has happened, and scared half to death
Of the silent one who each night creeps
Through to the bedroom and fitfully sleeps
'Til morning comes. With the new day
He is up again and again goes his way!

Never a word to the little brown house
Of why everything is quiet as a mouse!

Little brown house, I've good news for you!
You aren't forsaken. Their dream has come true!
Very soon now you can scarcely contain
The gladness and joy soon to be your domain!
Little brown house, you'll be happy to learn
That two went away but three will return!

The Troubles of Kirby

What you see here is the kid in-between
Who carries in dirt and carries out pie
I'm the only one who's horrid and mean
When I tell you, you won't wonder why –

My neck is so black, hair always on end
My teeth as unscrubbed as my shoes
Wonder why? I'm telling you friend
Mornings at our house there's no time to lose.

I slide out of bed and rush to a door
That always is closed in my face,
I hammer and pound, believe me I'm sore
Cause sis is just in there arranging her lace.

When she is done my stupid big bum
Of a brother has pushed me aside
Then it is late and I have to run
Believe me, it's hurtin' my pride.

So I make a dive into what's close at hand
Whether it's striped or checkered or plain.
Two more jumps and outdoors I land
Combing my hair with my fingers again.

Thoughts at Easter Time

Jesus, standing on a hill
That overlooked a sleeping town,
Saw pictured there a heavy cross
Saw also there a crown.

His heart ached for the cross that man
Devised in thought and deed.
Built it strong with lust and hate
With prejudice and selfish greed.

On Christ's great mission to the earth,
The pattern for a crown he brought,
He gave to us the jewels and gold
With which perfection might be wrought.

To fashion it He taught the way,
But each must make his own,
From golden hours a golden crown,
Each virtuous deed a precious stone.

From emeralds of faith, sapphire too
Here and there some diamond tears,
From topaz and rubies of love
A glorious crown for well spent years.

From a higher plane Christ stands today
A man of sorrow looking down
He weeps that man will choose a cross
When he might wear a crown.

Harvest Song

I love the harvests golden hue
October mornings crystal dew
I love the quiet sunny noon
I love October's smiling moon

I love my shelves where row on row
My labors like canned sunshine glow.
Sunsets of beet and kidney bean
High noon of carrots in between.

Borrowed from the summers grass
Dills and sweets smile out thru glass.
The grand tomato I suppose
Is reminiscent of a lovely rose.

There are berries from a blue, blue sky
And a purple cloud for a grape pie.
The lovely hued green beans and peas
Are colored like tall summer trees.

Fat cheeked peaches sweet and ripe
Golden globes from a bubble pipe
Blown by a boy on a summer day
Are perched here on my shelves to stay.

From the sheen of a summer star
Or from quiet streams that wonder far
Quarts of silver are gathered there
Sweet applesauce and Bartlett pear.

Ah, precious family I can't express
This all-consuming happiness
As I, like Midas, count my gold
And put it in your hands to hold.

This is my pledge of love for you
This is my dream in spring, come true
That we meet the winter well fortified
When the wind and snow will rage outside

~Summer of '52

Contemplations of the Future

We all will come to the bend in the road.
Some will go quickly, others linger a time
What is beyond is yet unknown
Whether a river to cross or a hill to climb

Our possessions remain this side of tomorrow
We go lightly around the bend in the road
If our treasures proceed us our hearts are there too
And we leave very little when we lay down our load

We never were promised all sunshine and gain
Nor were we destined for lives of all sorrow
But we'll know, intermingled they make life complete
When we go around the bend to tomorrow.

To Rev. Lloyd Hall

I am a robot
I am the perfect Methodist minister
I have a panel of buttons
No matter when, day or night
When a button is pushed, I am at your service
I am incapable of love, so don't love me—just push a button
My armor is impervious to darts and spears
They glance off and are harmless
To the delicate mechanisms contained in my shell
Questions are computerized
I always come up with the right answers
You may stand me on my head
Or kick me in the shins, it doesn't hurt
A robot just keeps going on
For I am a robot
I am the perfect Methodist minister

Alas, I am not a robot
I am not perfect
I have no panel of buttons
I am not always right
I am not wired for responses
I am a man made in the image of God
I live, I breathe, I enjoy life
I am a messenger from God
The words I speak, He gave to me for you
I rejoice in your happiness
And cry with you in sorrow

I baptize you, marry you and bury you
Always directing you toward Heaven
I love harmony and forbearance
And pray we will both be better Christians for having known each
other
I am your down to earth, striving for perfection, imperfect Methodist
minister.

The Place for Me

There's only one place in the world for me
'Tis the only place where real pleasure I see
'Tis a spot where everyone is loving and kind
And I feel not forsaken and left behind.

'Tis not a palace, rich and grand
Where wealth speaks on every hand
'Tis not a great king's marble hall
Oh, no, it's not like this at all.

The place for me is a long road
Where millions pass to their abode
Where the rich and poor I daily see
Oh, yes, this is the place for me.

Close by the road is my dwelling place
Where smiles spread over each happy face
When father returns from his daily toil
There we watch and wait in our cottage royal

Yes, this is my home, full of love and light
To it I'll ever turn my steps with delight
And hurry on full of joy and glee
For I know they're all waiting with welcome for me.

~Written in a sad mood, after my bosom friend deserted me to
look for other friends (Alfreda Dennis—age 17).

My Dream

I had a wonderful dream last night
    I dreamed of Galilee
I dreamed I walked with my Savior there
    And he lovingly smiled on me.
I followed close in his footsteps
    I left the world behind
He gently took me by my hand
    A better friend I could never find.

I walked with him in the morning
    We walked in the garden of light
Even the dewdrops seemed full of joy
    And I was in rapturous delight.
We walked on, mid nodding flowers
    They bowed at the Savior's feet
And the hundreds of birds in leafy bowers
    Seemed his name to repeat.

After the morning had faded away
    And noon had also passed
The shadows of evening were drawing
    And night was coming fast
I clung more closely to my Lord
He guided me through the stillness that came
Then a hush; and darkness prevailed
    And I heard him speak my name.

I opened my eyes and lo, I stood
Just outside the city of gold
The heavenly portals then opened wide
And my joys were a hundred fold
There hung, with my name above it
A crown on the jasper wall
It was filled with a thousand stars
And they were all mine-all.

I walked in Heaven and with him there
I tread the streets of gold
I found my friends on the golden stair
Our joys were untold
I longed for nothing, I was content
Up there with the millions on high
Then I awakened and resolved to live
A life fitted for that home in the sky.

*~ Written during revival meeting at the Markle Church of the
Brethren. The next Sunday I gave it in front of a large audience.
This is my mother's favorite of all my literary glimmers (Hilda
Alfreda Dennis—age 16).*

My Epitaph

When I am gone
Don't say that I'm dead;
Or grieve that hard earth
Is my final bed—for—

Dear Mother Nature's
Tucked me under her wing,
To wait for the morning
Of eternal spring.

May Day

I sit me down in early May,
I shut the noisy world without;
I give myself to sight and sound
Of the little world that lies about.

Glistening umbrella of lambs tongue
Makes a tiny spot of shade;
To hover o'er a ground birds nest
Where three small eggs are laid.

A brown leaf straining in the breeze,
Caught and held against its will;
Flutters goody-bye to wind bent grass
Marching o'er a sunlit hill.

Florescent clouds pinned to azure blue
By a naked thorn tree to detain;
While coaxing, begging it not to leave
'Til it gives us of its rain.

The earthwarm farmer plies his trade
Aerating the soil with watchful care;
Around the tiny thread like roots,
Which feed that lovely violet there.

Everywhere small spears of green
Pierce through dead, brown earth;
Each a Christ who breaks his tomb,
To proclaim God's promise of rebirth.

Then, I can at each day's close;
Cast off the shadows and at morn,
Arise refreshed to face my task,
Each day, God's child reborn.

Here I seek and here I find
My soul o'er runs with cheer;
For in this Eden on the earth,
My God and I hold Council here.

Day's Close

When the long gray shadows of evening
Play tag with gold in the west;
When the sun sinks away as though hiding,
Comes the hour that I love the best.

When the night folds its arms for protection,
And lulls all its creatures to sleep,
I take my post by the window,
And alone there my vigil I keep.

Supper is ready, fire is turned low;
The kettles contented to purr,
My work is done; now as I rest
I watch and wait for my "Sir."

Again he's arrived, he raises his hand
In greeting to me waiting there;
I hurry to do all the last minute things,
Hurry the children, no time to spare.

If we'd nail up a sign over our door,
I'm sure that we are agreed;
As we gather around with our darlings again,
"God Blessed Our Home," it would read.

To a February Snowdrop

Dear little flower, you are early,
First little blossom of spring!
As I kneel down to greet you I worry,
You seem such a wee, tender thing!

You must know how happy you make me,
By coming this particular day;
When my heart is aching with sadness,
Longing for one who's away.

I have always looked up to see angels,
But today when I suddenly found,
You smiling at me, my sweet angel,
I knew they come, too, from the ground.

I know, too, who sent you, sweet flower,
Your message is plain as can be;
And I love the dear God who remembered
A meek, humble creature like me.

I'll tuck brown leaves closer for shelter,
To protect you as long as you stay;
Your message I'll treasure forever,
This hope you have brought me today.

To a Rose

There's no spot in the world
Where God is so near
As among his sweet flowers
Where falls on my ear
His soft voice. My heart listens
And can scarcely contain its ecstasy.
Ah, Heaven's most surely a beautiful place!
My garden portends it! Some day
When at last I look on God's face
I shall know him! My heart knows
That I shall have seen him
Many times in a rose!

Vast Heritage
(October in Indiana)

Nature's richest gifts surround us
More gold than heart or hand can hold
Priceless rubies in autumn sunsets
Diamond stars onyx nights enfold!

Silver wings of air bourn insects
Streak across the autumn sun
Beneath the trees, await for children
Piles of bronze and crimson fun.

Parachutes escape the weed patch
Asparagus has turned to gold
Summer silent mums are singing
A color chorus before the cold!

What wondrous wealth we mortals own!
Too priceless for mere purse or 'roll
It will remain our own forever
Within the vaults of heart and soul

Old Garden Hat

It has never been to Sunday school
Or to a fancy tea
It has never gone to dinner
Or on a shopping spree

It was never to a party
Or fancy things like that
This old, old friend of mine
My faded garden hat.

When we go out together
I am where I love to be
Digging in my garden
Where my heart is light and free.

Where the wind caresses softly
Where enchanted voices sing
There we love to be together
My old hat and me and spring.

To a Grandson

I know a little fellow
With a dimple on his chin
Who sets the place to humming
Soon as he comes in!

He's such a little fellow
No bigger than a minute
But he rules the roost most surely
And all the people in it.

His Grandpa entertains him
By waggling his tongue
And making funny noises
Like a hen does to her young!

His uncle runs and "fetches"
Bottles, toys and whatnot
For his majesty who's waiting
His daily cruise in taylor-tot.

His Grandma loves and pets him
Hoping all the while
That she will be rewarded
With a two-toothed smile!

When his baby face turns upward
Smiling eyes are bright
And chubby arms say, "Take me!"
The whole world's right!

Sometimes I get disgusted
With this old world today
But so long as there are babies
I guess I'd like to stay!

A September Day

Nostalgic days are these again
And I can scarce express
The deep emotion in my soul
Like an aching happiness!

Be it my lot to ever live
When sight and sound have gone
May I have captured of this day
Memories to feed upon!

Memories like the humming bird
That feeds from bush and vine
Memories like the little song
From this happy lad of mine.

Of the winds wild escapades
Between these pages. Turning then
To ruffle up the feathers
Of my one white hen.

Memories of my guardian
In whose brown eyes I see
Communication of his love
Though his lips can't speak to me.

Lacy patterns on the lawn
Where the maples shadow falls
Too delicate to duplicate
Patterns never in "McCall's."

The pageant of rare loveliness
Of all the flowers in bloom
Will surely come when I recall
My outdoor living room!

If I MUST come to lonely days
Oh, may I then remember
To feed my hungry soul upon
Sights and sounds, which were
September!

A Soliloquy

'Tho miles and miles divide us
And your face I cannot see
As I sit by the fire, in the lamplight
Sweet memories come drifting to me.

'Tho it won't be long 'til the week ends
Yet I'm awful lonesome and blue,
And my thought like doves in the air
Are swiftly flying over you.

~ "Fritz" at letter time to Elmer.

To Elmer

Once our hearts together lay
On cupids burning shrine
The fire of love soon melted them
And your heart ran to mine.

Cupid saw from where he sat
And thought he'd have some fun
He quickly cooled the shrine and left
Our hearts forever one.

~ Written for Elmer on Valentine's Day

November Woods

November woods are bare and cold
November winds are fierce and bold
Deep lie the leaves in shades of brown
In limp profusion on the ground.

The naked trees blend hues of gray.
Majestic sentinel who moan and sway
And seek reprieve with up stretched hands
From winters gripping icy bands.

No feathered songster o'erflow with mirth
No variety of color on the brown breast of earth
No chirruping, no buzzing, no sound at my feet
Only nutcracker peers from his lofty retreat.

Yet I know they're all there. Each in his way
Has prepared for himself a warm place to stay.
How infinite God's wisdom to remember them all
To clothe them, to feed them the great and the small.

So strange is this silence, so great it's appeal
So lasting its impression, it has made me feel
Deep within me a renewal a rebirth
As I commune with my God, through creations on earth.

To Those We Love

The pink, white, green and silver
Somehow turns to gold
Bringing a beautiful harvest
More than a heart can hold.

The fulfillment of life's aspirations
Bring joy to this golden day
Mined from years of constant endeavor
Smiled upon by our Creator's assay.

Success, not measured by power or wealth
Proudly adorns these years of ease
We have contentment, love and joy
Who could ask for more than these?

We are proud of the fruits of our labor,
Our children and grandchildren too,
What ever there is of good in us
Let it live on in you.

~Love Dad and Mom
  (Written for our 50th wedding anniversary dinner at the
  Gateway Inn in 1980).